What individuals are saying about The Tax People. . .

"Over 99% of the time, we are able to resolve audits and issues and the taxpayer never has to personally meet with the IRS."

> — **Mr. Jesse Cota**, National Director of Taxes
> for The Tax People talking about
> TTP's retroactive audit protection services

"I had lost all my receipts and the IRS agreed to let my tax return go as is."

> — **Art Hebner**, talking about the outcome
> of a recent audit where he was
> represented by The Tax People

"I feel that within three years, The Tax People will be the household name in the tax industry, just as H&R Block was in the last decade."

> — **Larry Stocker**, TTP's Creative Director
> comparing his experiences
> launching other name brands

"I believe so highly in The Tax People that I am a member using the tax-saving strategies and services."

> — **Judge Richard Dahms**, former
> Missouri Assistant Attorney General

"Using the Tax Relief System, my CPA amended my past returns. I am $21,000 ahead in tax savings by purchasing the $300 Tax Relief System."

> — **Troy Helming**, member of The Tax People

"The Tax People showed my parents how to legally save $18,000 in capital gains taxes on a property sale."

— **Sarah Guetschow,** Vice Pres. Women Masterminds

"The Tax People serve the large and growing number of Americans who are placing a very high priority on legally reducing taxes paid and who want excellent audit protection via the present U.S. Federal Tax Code."

— **Bill Helming,** highly-respected national economist and recognized by the Cato Institute, Washington D.C., as one of America's top fundamental tax reform experts.

"The Tax People's tax experts calculated an additional $100,000 in legal deductions that my CPA had missed. That additional $100,000 in write-offs at my 39% tax bracket means I saved $39,000 before I even made a penny with my TTP business!"

— **Patrick James,**
nationally respected investment expert

"By my third month in The Tax People, I was earning $7,700. By my ninth month, my income was $20,000 per month. At this growth rate, I should be making $40,000 a month by my 15th month in business. I'm not a tax expert. I simply enroll new customers who use The Tax People's customized, hands-on expertise to attain powerful results."

— **Kathy Coover,** talking about
her TTP home-based business

"After only seven months, I have a six-inch, three-ring binder full of check copies. I'm starting to fill the next binder. Every day I receive checks for $300, $600 and $900, sometimes up to six checks a day."

— **Arlene Agoncillo,** talking about her
home-based business income from
offering The Tax People services.

The Result is Money

TheTaxPeople.Net Phenomenon!

Lori Prokop

Who You Are International, Inc.

Published by

Who You Are International, Inc.

8510 Elmore Avenue

Webster, MN 55088

507-744-2097

cash@megabestseller.com

Copyright © 2000 by Lori Prokop

Printed in the United States of America

February, 2000

ISBN 1-56352-330-2

*Dedicated to Johnny Meadows,
who lived life with courage and vision*

Acknowledgments

Special thanks to my business partner and husband, Marty Prokop, who is one incredible person!

My gratitude and respect go out to our whole publishing team who does whatever it takes to accomplish our goals and timelines:

Stephen and David Lisi, cover design; Linda Cadwalader Gulbrandson, editorial; Dan Smith and Christina Killion, contributing writers; Lynne Cahoon, Stacy Moldaschel and Joyce Selover, transcriptions; and the many other important people on our publishing team.

Expressed gratitude to The Tax People's CEO Michael Cooper and his family. It has truly been my pleasure writing this story that first began with the Cooper family.

Thank you to the women and men at TTP's home office and in the field. The Tax People's Chamla Brown deserves a very special thank you for all her time and efforts. She is an incredible person. To Todd Strand, Johnny MacNaught and Jesse Cota: thank you for the insights, encouragement and editing. My gratitude to Steve Kassel and Jim Edwards for their guidance.

Sincere appreciation to TTP's Independent Marketing Associates who gave of themselves through their experiences and kindly shared their stories in this book.

Thank you to Curtis Burgess and Eileen Cohen whose support and encouragement is much needed and most appreciated.

Contents

The Result is Money

TheTaxPeople.Net Phenomenon!

Lori Prokop

Who You Are International, Inc.

FOREWORD

Jeff Schnepper is the author of How to Pay Zero Taxes *(17th edition, McGraw-Hill). He is Microsoft's tax expert for their Web site. He co-authored* Microsoft Money *and* Turbo Tax Deluxe.

Mr. Schnepper is one of America's most highly respected tax experts. He holds two law degrees and an MBA in finance. He is one of The Tax People's tax strategists and advisors verifying that the Tax Relief System *provides people with accurate and valid tax advice.*

When Michael Cooper launched The Tax People his mind was filled with anticipation and hope. However, he never dreamed that in slightly over two years, an entire book would be written about the results people across America are experiencing with the services of his company.

Before agreeing to become one of their select tax experts, I attended a TTP convention in Missouri with over 1,000 people present. What really impressed me was how TTP changed the lives of its customers. I saw people who went from the brink of poverty to earning massive checks on a monthly basis. I saw them with their families and children with tears of gratitude in their eyes. I could sense the feeling of family that Mike Cooper created with this company.

You'll meet many of those people in the pages that follow. Some have sophisticated backgrounds in finance and sales; for others this is their first entrepreneurial venture.

Even with different backgrounds, they all have a common bond: They ventured from their familiar worlds and into the unknown. This book is about making that move and the adventures and rewards that eventually follow. What will emanate is a vision of possible choices.

At times, these choices seem illogical. A single mother and her two teenage daughters saving people from the clutches of the IRS? A disabled man rescuing able-bodied people from financial death? A homeless couple helping wealthy individuals save money on taxes? You probably wouldn't have bet on any of them in the beginning.

That would have been your loss. Single parent Vita Silvio and her daughters spent part of their summer on the beaches of the Caribbean. When Greg Alexander's heart stopped and he lay unconscious in the hospital, his family's financial worries were resolved with the $2,400 monthly residual income that continued to be paid, regardless if he could work or not. Formerly homeless,

Tali and Josey Mauai are moving into a 3,200 square foot, $297,000 home in Hawaii.

Shocking? Absolutely. It's living proof that the unbelievable happens — every day, to ordinary folks. Yet, we're not talking fairy tales. No magic spells replace work and follow-through. Many of the people in this book have succeeded by doing more than they believed they could and aligning with an internal force more formidable than magic.

All people should find within themselves the courage to start and operate their own businesses. It provides a perspective on life that can't be found anywhere else. Entrepreneurship requires people to discover and test their human spirit. You don't have to be seasoned, wealthy or connected to succeed. Whether you realize it or not, you have everything it takes.

For the last 30 years, when completing my personal taxes, I have used the same home-based business strategies that The Tax People recommend. I have always had a home-based office and used those deductions every year on my tax return without question from the IRS. They are legitimate.

I have clients who pay me $500 an hour to tell them how to reduce their taxes. The reality is that taxpayers who can afford expensive professional tax planning don't pay high taxes.

The goal of The Tax People is to provide that planning and those techniques to taxpayers of all income levels.

Most don't even realize that they are overpaying. Supreme Court Justice Sutherland once remarked, "The legal right of a taxpayer to decrease his taxes or to altogether avoid them by means which the law permits cannot be doubted."

The Tax People is dedicated to that ideal. TTP offers the same level of service to the little guys that I've been selling to the big guys. TTP guarantees they will find you at least $5,000 in additional deductions during your first 12 months actively following its business plan or the company will return the money you have invested in their services.

TTP helps the people who need it the most — the middle class. Our taxes are being paid by the middle class. If I have a couple that is making $60,000 a year and I save them $5,000 a year, it's meaningful to them. If I have a couple making $2,000,000 and I save them $100,000 that year, they're happy; but their lifestyle hasn't been improved. I want to get the people who are making $30,000 year and turn them into people who are making $3,000,000 a year.

Everyone I have met who is a customer of TTP is raving about the tax savings, but there are more benefits than just tax savings. There is also wealth accumulation. People who are becoming customers of TTP and working it as businesses are making more money. As a result, the amount of taxes they are paying increases. I would rather make $100,000 keeping $90,000 paying $10,000 in taxes than make $10,000 keeping only $9,000 paying $1,000 in taxes. It's not just what you pay; it's how much *more* you can earn. I think that's the real advantage of The Tax People. They teach and provide each person the opportunity to raise his or her standard of living.

Most families are struggling financially because they are overpaying their taxes and understandably so. The tax code is extremely complicated and changes every year. I am a tax professional. The tax code is my life. I know how much I don't know. God help Americans who are not professional tax strategists or tax professors and are asked to translate the unintelligible tax code.

Before the changes in 1998, the IRS tax code was 9,471 pages containing 1,300,000 words. The 1997 tax regulations, which are needed to interpret the tax code, consist of 91,824 pages and 5,750,000 words. This is a total of 101,295 pages and over 7,050,000 words.

In comparison, the Bible has 1,291 pages. This means the Bible is 99,464 pages shorter than the tax code and regulations. To receive all the tax benefits that you are allowed by law, each year you would have to read, understand and retain 78 Bibles worth of information.

The 1998 changes have increased that amount. Every year the tax code and regulations grow bigger and more complicated. To fill out the 1040EZ tax form, the IRS sends you 31 pages of fine print instructions — and that's the easy form. The amount of paperwork and information is staggering. If I took all the tax returns and associated paperwork that the IRS receives, it would circle the globe 36 times every year.

Just imagine trying to defend yourself in an audit. It is imperative that all people have the audit defense provided by The Tax People. They know it and want it.

Read and enjoy the story of this amazing company. Put yourself into the shoes of the people who are using the services of The Tax People and building their TTP businesses. In the next year, your family could pay fewer taxes, make more money and enjoy more freedom than ever before in your life. Or, you could have the same monetary results this year as last — it's your choice. But either way, the RESULT *is* MONEY! Either YOURS or "t-h-e-I-R-S."

INTRODUCTION

*"This book will start by talking about money
and conclude by changing your life."*

— **Lori Prokop,** author of *The Result Is Money*

This is the story of The Tax People, a remarkable
home-based business opportunity. It's about people
helping people and the emotional and financial rewards
open to those who do. It's about a high-growth company
led by CEO Michael Cooper, a man whose reputation of
generosity, honesty and integrity is the basis for the
company's values. It's about you — how you can create
the wealth and lifestyle you desire.

What You Desire Also Desires You

Could that statement be true for you? It would be nice,
wouldn't it? What if it were true for you? What is it that
you would have?

Is it more time?

More money?

A new home?

To travel?

A new car?

To fund a cause to change the world?

Take a look at your list. Is it as long as it was when you were a teenager? Is it like the list you made when you were first out on your own — just *you* against the world? Are your wants and desires still dreamy or have they become more practical through the years?

The reality is that time shrinks most dreams to fit lives that are less than what people originally intended.

People who once dreamed of becoming President of the United States are now in charge of taking out the trash on Thursday nights. Others who wanted walk-in closets full of the latest fashions are now figuring out how to mix-and-match two suits and three shirts to create five days of wearing. Yet others who envisioned big homes are now living in duplexes that are too small for their growing families.

And what about the epidemic that sweeps our neighborhoods every weekday morning at 5:30? You can hear it coming: "buzzzzz, slam, buzzzzz, slam, buzzzzz, slam" as the alarm clocks ring. Children are left to fend for themselves as parents make mad dashes to join the standstill of rush-hour traffic.

See Dick and Jane race to the office on Monday morning. See them come home Monday night. See them race again Tuesday morning, come home Tuesday night; race again Wednesday morning, drag themselves home Wednesday night; race Thursday morning, drag Thursday night; race Friday morning, Friday night. Saturday morning over-time. Sunday night finds them getting ready for Monday at the office.

What happens to Dick and Jane after 25 or 30 years of this?

They're replacing tires because of too many miles, each other because of too many absences, and dreams because of too many sacrifices.

All for the illusion of someday having enough time. Their quest for life is killing them just when it should be rewarding them.

Finally, the "Dick and Janes" of America are discovering how to instantly buy back their time.

Often times, they are putting thousands of dollars a year back in their pockets and earning thousands more daily, weekly and monthly from the comfort of their own homes.

You can do the same. How?

You can immediately increase your net take-home pay without asking your boss for a raise. The Tax People will show you how to legally lower your income taxes in an easy-to-understand, hassle-free way. Step-by-step they will show you how to keep your money in your hands instead of overpaying it in taxes.

But Is It Really Legal?

The Tax People have based their *Tax Relief System* on information established by U.S. Tax Code and Regulations, IRS Revenue Rulings along with Tax and District Court Rulings. Over 1,000 tax professionals nationwide have fully endorsed the strategies outlined in the *Tax Relief System*. This proves the information is legal, valid and correct.

Substantial tax savings are legally created by transferring individuals' expenses from the category of non-deductible personal expenses to tax-deductible business expenses.

Using The Tax People's tax-saving strategies, people can legally receive immediate, sustaining net take-home pay raises of as much as $100 per week. Two-income families often realize immediate increases of $300 to $900 per month and more.

Scott Turner, the leading tax expert for a legal firm with 5.2 million clients, talks about taxpayers *without* the services of The Tax People: "In reality, many of these taxpayers are and have been over-paying their taxes by 30% and more."

Think about how your life would improve if thousands of dollars were put back in your pocket for you to do as you wish.

Why Hasn't Anyone Thought Of This Before?

The Tax People idea was conceived in 1997 when Michael Cooper had a brief conversation with a former IRS agent who had turned high-price tax guru. The expert pointed out how Mr. Cooper had lost $250,000 worth of deductions and had overpaid his taxes by more than $50,000 over the course of 10 years.

Having both majored in business and accounting in college and instructed thousands of people on home-based tax deductions, Cooper thought that he had his personal taxes under control. It took only minutes to discover information beyond what Michael ever thought possible. Immediately, he wanted more of this tax expert's valuable advice, but realized at $1,000 an hour, it was not affordable to small, home-based or even mid-sized businesses.

The Tax People (TTP) was born to make high-level tax advice and audit protection available to all American entrepreneurs and employees.

Cooper summarizes, "Any knowledgeable tax expert will tell you that the best tax strategy, whether for professional white collar executives or blue collar employees, is a home business. The first problem is that most people don't know how to set up a home business that will actually generate income. Second, home business owners don't know what tax deductions they can take and, most of the time, neither do their CPA's. TTP solves both these challenges.

"TTP provides the only business opportunity that I am aware of which *guarantees* people will come out ahead. Our tax strategies can increase people's take-home pay by $400 a month or more."

The Tax People guarantee in writing that following their simple business plan will provide you with at least $5,000 in additional legal tax deductions or TTP will refund the fees paid for services. That's a more-than-fair guarantee.

Are Taxpayers Really Doing This?

November of 1998, The Tax People boasted approximately 2,000 clients, all of whom had access to the tax expertise and audit protection services. Within 18 months that figure exploded to over 20,000. That's just the tip of the iceberg according to CEO Cooper: "All 120,000,000 American taxpayers are ideal candidates for our tax expertise and audit protection."

TTP's parent corporation, Renaissance, Inc. was formed January, 1995. TTP was incorporated and started offering tax expertise and audit protection services in November, 1997. It has become the largest and fastest growing non-franchised tax service in America. In just 24 months, sales have grown 1200% and the company projects annualized revenues by the end of 2000 to reach $100,000,000. The company is on a growth curve similar to Microsoft's.

In addition to individuals, tax professionals nationwide are joining the company in volume and, in many cases, greatly increasing the gross incomes of their practices by becoming TTP affiliated offices. For tax professionals, their incomes are increased by preparing taxes according to TTP's system. Audit protection remains in the hands of The Tax People. Professionals love this because most hate audits as much as their clients.

Other professionals such as attorney Mary Joe Smith are also interested in TTP. Mrs. Smith, a former Missouri Assistant Attorney General for six years, currently operates her own growing private practice. She looked over TTP's services with her clients in mind and decided to join as a customer, herself.

Mrs. Smith confirms, "I have several hundred clients sleeping better at night. Once we got the fear of tax deductions, returns and audits out of their lives, they became better business people — more creative. They became better moms and dads because many of their fears and money worries are gone. If a person has money worries, they can't do anything else. It stifles their creativity and initiative.

"There is no place that I know of that has this kind of protection and information. There is no course in high school that teaches this. There's no course in college or law school that teaches the unreadable tax code boiled-down to 52 simple-to-understand pages. In addition, you receive audit protection, tax preparation and the network of experts who you can personally call and rely on."

Home Is Where The Business Is

In this book, you'll read about people across America who are replacing some or all of their J-O-B incomes with profits generated by their home-based TTP businesses. Many seasoned business owners are discovering TTP businesses can outpace previous return-on-investments.

All this is happening from the comfort of people's homes.

Home-based business is no longer a fancy trend for people on the edge. It's become a way of life for even the most traditional members of society.

Recently, I interviewed the *New York Times* best-selling author of *The Roaring 2000's* and *The Roaring 2000's Investor*, investment strategist and economic futurist Harry Dent. I asked him, "Are Americans better off working for themselves or staying as employees and investing in the stock market?"

Here's what he told me: "I'm getting a greater return out of my own home-based business than investing. In my profession, I have a lot of investing options. The market will provide an easy return of 14% to 20% for the next 5 to 10 years. But, for a lot of people the important issue is, 'I need to do something with my life. I'm getting out of my corporate position. I want to start a business that can sustain me.'"

This book reveals how Americans are doing more than sustaining. They are cashing in their corporate struggles, slowing down and living healthier, wealthier lives.

To achieve their new lifestyles, they are teaming up with a group of brilliant leaders who have formed a remarkable company offering life-changing services and protection.

Possibly even more remarkable is that, up to this point, Americans have learned about The Tax People solely through word-of-mouth from current customers. Each customer has a financial stake in The Tax People's overall success. Tens of thousands of people have joined as a unified team of home-based business owners to promote and build the company while sharing in the revenues created. *The result is money* — and it's available to you, too.

You Make A Living By What You Receive; You Make A Life By What You Give

"One person can make a difference and every person should try."

— **John F. Kennedy**

A success larger-than-life rose from the center of Michael Cooper's being. It was more a knowing in the pit of his stomach than a picture in his mind's eye. He knew that to pull it off, he needed an extraordinary reason for its success. He found it in his business partner, Johnny Meadows.

He first met Johnny when Michael was a consultant for a large company in North Carolina. They were strangers to each other when Johnny walked through the company's front door, past the reception desk and straight to Michael's office. After a brief, impromptu interview, Johnny looked directly into Michael's eyes with an intense certainty and announced, "I'm going to work for you. I want to work here and I'm going to work for *you*." Taken aback and somewhat amazed, Michael agreed and hired the energetic young man on the spot for an open warehouse position.

Later, Michael left the employ of the company and contacted Johnny with an offer. "I've got a new job for you as my partner. Here are the terms. To start with, all the money is going back into our company. I'm not going to draw a salary and neither are you. You can live with my family and me. I've got an extra car you can drive. I can give you pocket change for spending money. If we fail, you are gambling three months. If we succeed, you can rise to whatever level you can handle, from janitor to president. Whatever position you occupy, I will overpay you in that role because you gambled on us."

Michael paused before he continued, "So, Johnny, are you willing to bet three months . . . on us?"

Johnny hopped the next plane to Kansas where he and Michael Cooper founded a consulting firm that specialized in training independent representatives for several dozen network marketing companies. Michael continues, "I told Johnny that he had an unlimited opportunity. It was just he and I starting this show."

Michael figured that after three months either Johnny would be able to earn more money than he would anywhere else or their team would have failed.

Michael and Johnny succeeded in providing training and consultation to thousands of independent distributors, as well as, various network marketing companies. Under their guidance, several enterprises grew over $100,000,000 in sales. Michael explains, "As the sales figures increased, so did the owners' greed and carelessness. They hired us to develop and build their companies. Then a turning point arrived where the money was rolling into the bank and they stopped paying distributors."

Michael decided enough was enough. After watching the owners' carelessness ruin those opportunities, he decided to separate himself from their companies. After more than 10 years guiding other network marketing companies, Michael again asked Johnny to become his partner in a new venture. Together, they launched their own network marketing enterprise, Renaissance, Inc.

Three years into their new company, their many successes had created new opportunities. Michael explains, "We decided to expand to include a tax services division called Advantage International Marketing (AIM), which later evolved into TheTaxPeople.net. It was November 5, 1997 when we had an AIM business presentation scheduled in the Kansas City area at the home of Kent McLaughlin, a new AIM customer. Johnny and I were excited because after years of hard work, we were truly watching our dreams become realities.

"Our big day arrived. Uncharacteristically, Johnny had not come to work that morning. He hadn't even called. By afternoon, I was extremely concerned and had a real uneasy feeling. We called his house and his parents back in North Carolina. We just couldn't locate him."

Michael knew Johnny would never miss an important business presentation. They had invested years toward this day. Michael recounts: "I was first hoping that Johnny had simply overslept. By afternoon, I was really concerned. He always showed up for work unless he called. Finally, I asked one of the staff members to stop by Johnny's to make sure everything was okay as I needed to go ahead and leave for Kent's home for the presentation."

Traveling along Interstate 70, the hypnotic hum of the tires soothed Michael's mind. He navigated the highway as his thoughts traveled forward to the evening event. He envisioned the outcome and a feeling of accomplishment warmed his heart. It spread a grateful smile across his face. Michael knew their company was ready for its new growth.

His peace was interrupted by the piercing ring of his car phone. As Michael placed the receiver to his ear, his mind raced back to the moment in an effort to comprehend what he was being told. The voice pleaded, "Michael, are you driving? Pull over. It's about Johnny."

Instantly, Michael's smile was erased as he simultaneously took a deep breath. His muscles tensed as he heard soundless pain echoing through the phone. Michael clenched his teeth and braced for the oncoming news. Fighting to control his worst fears, he asked, "Is he all right? Where is he?"

Unwelcomed reticence followed as if respectful silence would momentarily heal what was about to be said. The eerie hush was shattered. "Michael, I'm really sorry...," as the voice dropped-off. "They found Johnny in his apartment. Michael, I'm so sorry. He died this morning."

The cell phone dropped, his thoughts whirled in violent circles of disbelief, anger and sorrow. Michael gasped for air as his mind reached a dizzy exhaustion and stomach churned nauseously.

Through blinding tears, Michael searched for the edge of the interstate where his car and his hopes were brought to an abrupt halt. His Town Car shook from the waves of vehicles rushing past him, as he sat alone among billows of people.

Michael realized that just as their success had begun, it also had ended.

He was alone again. This wasn't Michael's first loss. When he was 25, he survived the pain of his wife's passing. She left two living treasures to Michael's care, the precious, young children they cherished.

Now, Michael was dealing with the incurable pain of losing another best friend, a partner who had now left their fledgling venture to Michael's guidance.

Through his pain, Michael cried a prayer into the depths of his soul: "What would Johnny want me to do?"

His mind rationalized that Michael had every reason to turn home, but his heart felt every reason to move forward. The internal struggle continued until the strength of his heart gave Michael the power to move his car into the flow of traffic. Michael knew Johnny would continue driving east towards Kent McLaughlin's house.

When Michael arrived, he informed Kent that, only hours earlier, a heart attack had taken Johnny's 32-year-old life. Shocked, Kent offered and expected Michael to cancel the meeting.

However, Michael had already made peace with his decision, "Johnny would want me to build this company. He knows that his parents and brothers now own his share. More than anything, right now, he's depending on me to take care of his family."

The success of that AIM presentation became apparent when 20 of the 21 people attending became customers. The host, Kent McLaughlin, went on to become a millionaire as one of AIM's, and The Tax People's, top money-earners. That night, through his pain, Michael Cooper cultivated the seeds that thousands of families, including Johnny's, will continue to harvest for years to come.

The Greatest Good We Can Do For Others Is Reveal Their Riches

Curtis Burgess, one of the very first people to join Michael and Johnny in those early days, is among the many Independent Marketing Associates who are now gratefully harvesting golden crops with their home-based businesses. Curtis is one of The Tax People's top-level producers having earned the much-desired title of Diamond and an on-going portion of the total financial success of the company.

Prior to his financial success with The Tax People, Mr. Burgess owned four businesses where the 24 hour, 7 day a week work and worry over company-related problems were taking their toll on him and his family. For over 25 years, Mr. Burgess owned and operated an auto parts store, a used car lot, a full-service insurance agency and an automotive chemical distributorship.

Commenting on his prior businesses, "They were all very time, employee, stress and investment-intensive with little return."

Just two years into his TTP home-based business, the *monthly* five-figure income it generates has afforded Curtis the luxury of selling two of his cash-poor, energy-zapping companies with the other two also for sale.

Mr. Burgess reflects, "I couldn't sell my high overhead businesses before, even though they weren't the best. They gave me some form of mental security and income."

"The beautiful part about starting my home-based business was that I could stay in my comfort zone with my other businesses while I built my TTP business.

When I started, I had the fear of the unknown. I couldn't give up what I had in order to build something new."

After a year in his TTP business, Burgess walked out of his auto parts store and told his son, "If you can't run this, we're putting it on the auction block."

The security of a TTP business provided the Burgess family with an additional bonus. "Operating our auto parts store gave my son the opportunity to grow as a businessman because I was out of the picture. It was sink or swim. I'm proud to say he's swimming, but he has also decided to build a TTP business on the side."

Mr. Burgess continues, "Now that I have experienced how fast and profitable TTP businesses are, I wish I had done this full-time from day one. I believe my income would be three times larger than it is now."

Curtis claims a TTP business and its services are the only things in America that actually cost people more money *not* to own. According to Burgess, most of his customers who follow TTP's system realize over $5,000 per year in actual tax reduction. "That's a savings of over three times what it costs to be a customer for a whole year."

As Mr. Burgess reasons, "The money that you pay to be involved in TTP's audit protection and tax expertise services comes from a small part of what you would have paid the IRS anyhow but now keep in your pocket."

The monthly five-figure income that Mr. Burgess enjoys is beyond tax savings. It is actual positive cash-flow income from his home-based business profits and bonuses. Burgess' success was built from the word-of-mouth growth that the *Tax Relief System* is generating and the resulting profits from customers joining through his sales organization.

In Curtis' experience, 50-60% of the people who watch the company's video become customers. The nominal fees for the tax expertise and audit protection services create a residual income for people who introduce others to the tax system. In addition, customers who actively introduce others to the business have the opportunity to earn a bonus of a free car of their dreams. Some people qualify for their vehicle in their very first month.

Curtis proceeds, "Prior to the TTP tax system, people had to know something about taxes to get tax deductions. Now, just follow the system and you get tax breaks. You share your personal experience with others, give them a video and put them in touch with the Tax Dream Team."

Burgess details, "People considering TTP's services and those people's tax professionals can access the Tax Dream Team to verify that TTP's tax-saving system, expertise and claims are real." After people have become customers, they have direct access to the Tax Dream Team.

The Tax People has cleverly retained America's premier tax experts for people who, as individuals, could not have previously found these tax gurus or afforded their services.

As stated in the introduction, the idea was conceived in 1997 when CEO Cooper had a 10-minute chat with a former IRS agent who had turned high-price tax guru. The expert was in private practice after 28 years with the IRS. He pointed out how Mr. Cooper had lost $250,000 worth of deductions and had overpaid his taxes by more than $50,000 over the course of 10 years. "Enough money to send my children to college," Cooper sighed.

Having majored in business and accounting in college, then taught home-business taxes to thousands of people in network marketing, CEO Cooper thought that he had his personal taxes under control. It took only minutes with the tax expert to learn more than Michael ever thought possible. Immediately, he wanted more of this tax expert's valuable advice, but realized at $1,000 an hour, it was not affordable to small, home-based or even mid-sized businesses.

Money Never Starts An Idea. It's The Idea That Starts The Money.

Thanks to Michael and Johnny's entrepreneurial creativity, TTP was born to make high-level tax advice and audit protection available to all American entrepreneurs and employees.

Cooper summarizes, "Any knowledgeable tax expert will tell you that the best tax strategy, whether for professional white collar executives or blue collar employees, is a home business. The first problem is that most people don't know how to set up a home business that will actually generate income. Second, home business owners don't know what tax deductions they can take and, most of the time, neither do their CPA's. TTP solves both these challenges.

"TTP businesses are the only business opportunity that I am aware of which *guarantees* people will come out ahead. On average, our tax strategies increase a person's take-home pay by $400 a month or more."

Michael theorizes, "What if my mother, my minister and my very best friend became customers of The Tax People? What if they all failed miserably as business owners and never earned a profit or a single bonus check? The worst case scenario for customers of The Tax People would be that they are able to take, on average, additional tax deductions of about $5,000 or more by just intending to make a business profit."

Internet Excellence

Thousands of people agree with Michael Cooper as evidenced by the 23% monthly growth in TTP's customer base and over 69,000 daily hits to its Web site.

Although computers are not necessary for the success of their businesses, these current and prospective customers have access to the most user-friendly Web site in the home-business industry. Web master Eric Hill promises, "At our Web site, www.thetaxpeople.net, customers find every tool they need to succeed."

At any time, Independent Marketing Associates (IMA's) can access information about their businesses including sales volumes and bonus checks already on the way to their mailboxes. Eric reports, "The first year on-line our Web site experienced over 13,860,000 hits. My responsibility is to cater to the people who want to build their Tax People businesses with their computers."

The Web site also provides customers with a chat room and business training, both of which are real-time interactive. Eric explains, "We have 18 hours per week of on-line training which is also available on conference calls. People can choose business support via their computers or their phones. Both are free of charge."

The 24-hour support and detailed training have resulted in very noticeable advantages for TTP's Independent Marketing Associates. John MacNaught, Vice President of Field Operations for The Tax People, explains, "Traditionally, in network marketing as an industry, only a small minority of people who work their businesses actually earn measurable results. On average, as little as 2% to 5% of all network marketers actually make any money."

Mr. MacNaught describes the success of TTP customers: "Last month, 45% of our active Independent Marketing Associates earned checks. That's an incredibly large percentage of people making money. No other network marketing company can honestly claim results that high."

John says, "Network marketing statistics reveal that less than 15% of distributors stay involved and purchase the company's products. Retention of distributors has always been a challenge for network marketing companies. Most companies quote their retention numbers from one month to the next. This means that as people drop during one month, someone can replace them the next month without affecting the retention rate. This creates a false picture of retention."

Mr. MacNaught explains that TTP figures the retention of its Independent Marketing Associates as actual people from year-to-year. He states, "The question is, 'Did Sally and Dave join and are they still with us?' Companies who enroll people and treat them as faceless numbers are doing a disservice. We want to know that the 'Sallys' and 'Daves' of the world are becoming customers, experiencing success, making money and staying here to build their TTP businesses."

John continues, "The Tax People has a two-year retention rate of over 72%. That's five to ten times industry average. Several positive factors cause people to stay active with The Tax People.

"First, as a result of starting their own TTP businesses, people receive immediate net take-home pay increases by following our tax experts' advice and increasing their W-4 deductions to account for their new business deductions.

"Second, people want to keep that money, so they want to keep their businesses active.

"Third, the increase in take-home pay could be $400 per month, per person. For a two-income earning family that could be $800. The nominal fee for the tax-saving strategies and audit protection is $100 a month. This means that families can increase their net cash flows by $700 even before we talk about the increase in overall income possibilities from their new home-based businesses."

Agreeing with Mr. MacNaught's first-hand experience is Christa Moussa, TTP's Director of Operations. She has been with The Tax People since its origin. "When TTP started, we were all hopeful toward future growth. We knew our timing was right. If you recall, 1997 was just before the Congressional hearings conducted into the functions of the IRS. Certain areas of the IRS were coming to light, particularly those that were not treating the American public as gently as they could. The national media had brought the fear of the IRS to the public eye."

Christa recounts, "Fortunately, just ahead of this time, we assembled a powerful team of ex-IRS agents turned pro-taxpayers and offered current and retroactive audit protection on tax returns — whether we had prepared them or not. We offered legal ways for families to reduce their taxes, even guaranteeing our customers that we would show them a minimum of $5,000 in additional deductions, or we'd return the money they had paid for our services.

"It was the right combination at the right time. As a result, just 24-months into our tax services expansion, our corporate gross income has grown by 1200% topping $3,000,000 a month. "

The Tax People, A Household Name

Larry Stocker, The Tax People's Creative Director, has witnessed the success that can result from this type of growth. He heads TTP's internal graphic and design department. Prior to his position with TTP, Larry had extensive experience as he had worked for a Kansas City advertising agency and for various firms on Chicago's Michigan Avenue.

Larry comments, "Prior to TTP, I'd been part of creative teams who had developed new products and services into some of today's most popular name brands. Our creative team here is taking the same steps with The Tax People. I feel that within three years, this new company will be the household name in the tax industry just as H&R Block was in the last decade.

"The Tax People is growing at hyper-speed. Internally, I see stability because of the company's growth and marketing potential. If somebody wanted to join this company as an employee and retire in 20 years, that is a reality."

Larry proceeds, "Having an internal advertising agency is significant and cost-effective only for stable companies of significant size. Consider your local dry cleaning business, the one that has been in your neighborhood for years. It may be stable, but it lacks the revenues needed to support an internal advertising agency.

"Only major corporations like pharmaceutical companies, financial organizations and larger insurance corporations have internal creative departments like ours. A company's revenue and workload must grow to a certain magnitude where an internal creative department is cost effective."

The Money Is There

To verify financial magnitude, simply talk to the accounting department. Nizar Tabet is an Accounting Specialist for The Tax People. He has been with the company since March 1999 and describes his daily functions: "I reconcile and deposit the company's daily income."

Nizar reveals, "My job has been getting harder and harder every day. The income has been growing so rapidly that working full-time, I can't keep up. We have hired an additional accounting assistant to handle deposits. There will be two of us, full-time, just controlling and depositing the growing daily cash flow."

When asked about the company's growth, Nizar comments, "This company has been growing fast. With rapid growth, companies usually have trouble with cash and maintaining healthy balance sheets. From what I have seen in the accounting department, we are growing really fast yet maintaining very healthy finances. TTP's cash flow is strong and is projected to continue to be strong. We have been insulated from the usual financial challenges of a growing company. For IMA's who are expecting checks, the money is there."

Wayne Keeling, TTP's Art Director since July 1998, faces the company growth on a daily basis. He is responsible for printed publications and graphics. "When I first started, I thought we were working at a fast-pace. Now we live in a super fast-pace. I love it. I've witnessed an incredible growth rate that will continue for years because our market potential has not even been tapped. At the rate that we are growing, I see us bigger than H & R Block and any other tax preparation company in a relatively short period of time."

When asked about the level of stress that a high-growth company can produce and the demands made on his time and talents, Wayne contemplates, "I've never had a boss that has been more down-to-earth, understanding and willing to work with employees than Mike Cooper. What has been most noticeable to me is how Mike handles himself. He really listens well. While he is a great communicator, he doesn't like to see his picture or hear himself talk. Working in the past with ego-centered executives, I thought overbearing personalities were the 'CEO norm.' Mike is not that way. He is easy to get along with because he first cares about other people."

Wayne says, "Even though everyone here works at hyper-speed, the environment is relaxing. Mike has developed an atmosphere where we all have the opportunity to speak and be heard. He has created a highly-dedicated team all working toward the same goals."

The Best Minute You Spend Is The One You Invest In Others

Viewed as a national expert on building and motivating teams, Major General James Rueger was nominated to the post of 2-Star Army General by President Bush. After his retirement from federal ranks, General Rueger was appointed by the Kansas governor as Commanding General of the state's 9,000 member Army and Air National Guards. He is now a customer of The Tax People.

When asked about how he ranks CEO Cooper, the General confirms, "Mike Cooper could be in my unit any time. I would bring him in as chief-of-staff. He is a motivator and has the best interests of the people in mind. The services and opportunity Mike has created with his TTP team are incredible — helping and saving lives."

The General recently retired from his state position as he explains, "When people spend that much time working every day of the year, they don't just shut off. I wanted to be busy. After helping adults and children for years, I could see where the services of The Tax People were something American people deserved."

Even though General Rueger had been a part of the United States government for decades, he still needed help understanding all the tax benefits available. "I've been a customer of The Tax People since May 1999. During my first six months, I saved $4,500 in taxes because of legal deductions that I never knew about."

Gene Boyd introduced his business-owner son, Matt, to The Tax People. The strategies and advice from TTP's tax experts legally saved Matt $17,000 on taxes the first year as a customer.

Entrepreneurial desire runs through Gene's family. He has been a Ford-Lincoln-Mercury car dealer for over a decade. In addition, he owned a Western Sizzlin Steakhouse business for 17 years and has invested in hotels and nursing homes. Prior to becoming a TTP customer in July 1998, Gene went through the same decision-making process that he used for all his other ventures.

"When I become involved in any new business there are several factors I consider. The first factor is the product. Is it of high quality and in high demand?

"In this case, people are looking for ways to legally reduce the amount of taxes they pay. Many families are going broke trying to pay their taxes. TTP offers immediate tax relief, unparalleled audit protection and solid tax-saving guidance to a potential market of 120,000,000 taxpayers and over 40,000,000 businesses. TTP can even help resolve IRS problems for taxpayers with levies, liens and unfiled tax returns in manners that are very favorable to taxpayers.

"When looking at a business venture, I always assess the risk. In the many businesses prior to The Tax People, I invested anywhere from $250,000 up to $800,000 with enormous risks. In those businesses not a single person guaranteed me any kind of income or savings. With TTP, customers have *NO* capital at risk. Even your minimal service fees are recouped in tax savings and are tax deductible as well! If you help three people become customers and they remain active, you've already earned more than twice the initial $300 cost of your *Tax Relief System.*

"The Tax People also provides you with a guarantee: If they can't legally and ethically find you an additional $5,000 in tax deductions, they'll return your money. Until I became an Independent Marketing Associate of The Tax People, I never had that kind of guarantee from any business.

"The next factor is the return-on-investment. As a Ford-Lincoln-Mercury dealer with millions of dollars at risk, I used to think 25% return on my investment was wonderful. After experiencing the return from my TTP business, I can confidently say that I did not know anything about return-on-investment before The Tax People.

"Here is what I've discovered. I'll use an example to illustrate. Assume the first month as a TTP customer, Mary pays the initial $300 for the *Tax Relief System.*

Then Mary provides $100 in each of the following 12 months for the audit protection and on-going tax strategies. Her first year costs would be $1,500. Mary is guaranteed to receive an additional $5,000 in legal tax deductions. Depending on Mary's tax bracket, that's a guaranteed tax-saving of up to $2,500 or more[1], because she'll probably realize $20,000 or more in deductions while actively working her new business.

"What Mary has found, as most customers do, is that they average $5,000 and more in *actual tax-savings*, not just deductions. Based on this experience, that's 333% return-on-investment through tax-savings alone.[2]

For two-income families the tax savings is often greater. Couples pay the same $1,500 first year for services, but can recoup double the tax savings at $10,000 or more for a return-on-investment of 667% on the tax savings alone.[3]

"Now, assume that Mary shares this legal tax-saving system with other people. Enrolling a few new customers each month plus a little organizational growth can quickly add up to $1,000 to $2000 per month based on part-time effort. These are very conservative figures. Multiply those monthly incomes by 12 months and Mary

---

[1] This figure is based on a 50% tax bracket. Other tax brackets can realize savings of different amounts.

[2] The return-on-investment has been rounded to the nearest one percent: $5,000 tax-savings / $1,500 investment = 333% return-on-investment.

[3] The return-on-investment has been rounded to the nearest one percent: $10,000 tax-savings / $1,500 investment = 667% return-on-investment.

is earning a part-time annual income of $12,000 to $24,000.

"Let's go back to Mary's annual tax savings of $5,000 and add it to her conservative part-time annual income figures of $12,000 to $24,000. Mary's $1,500 investment has just multiplied itself into between $17,000 and $29,000 in only one year.[4]

Gene booms, "That's a 1,133% to 1,933% return-on-investment![5]

"With the money-back guarantee customers receive, there is zero risk with incredible potential. You are 100% protected."

Gene consents, "At first people could think, 'This is too good to be true.' If I hadn't lived it myself, I might agree."

"In addition to first-hand experience, I've attended many Tax People business meetings that are open to all people interested in more information. It was at such a meeting where I met Two-Star Major General Rueger who is also a customer of The Tax People. I figured this guy is pretty sharp. He has connections in many places

---

[4] $5,000 tax-savings + $12,000 annual income = $17,000 total return and $5,000 tax-savings + $24,000 annual income = $29,000 total return.

[5] Each figure has been rounded to the one percent. $17,000 total return / $1,500 investment = 1,133% return-on-investment and $29,000 total return / $1,500 investment = 1,933% return-on-investment.

and is not going to jump into something without proper due diligence. Both of us are now enjoying great success with the company."

Gene confirms, "I also met Mary Joe Smith, former Missouri Assistant Attorney General, who is now a practicing attorney. Mrs. Smith assured me that she had completed her own legal due diligence on The Tax People. What were her findings? The company is so legal, stable and clean that she agreed to join The Tax People's Board of Directors. She is the second former Attorney General to sit on the board of TTP."

Approved By Judge Dahms

Missouri Judge Richard W. Dahms spent three years working in the Attorney General's office. He went on to become an assistant prosecuting attorney and was then elected into judgeship. After his retirement as a Missouri judge, Richard Dahms served as an attorney in private practice.

Judge Dahms talks about his affiliation with The Tax People: "I have been involved with The Tax People since its inception and sit on the Board of Directors. I believe so highly in The Tax People that I am also a customer using the tax-saving strategies and services."

Commenting on his personal experience with TTP's services, "I am just amazed at the benefits people can derive from being customers and following the guidance of The Tax People's experts. This tax-saving service has measured up with hundreds of CPA's who have blessed it. The company is on solid ground and has a history of reliability. I see everything good for The Tax People and its customers."

Talking about his observations as a board member, "I have not before seen a company grow this fast and do what this company has done in this short of a time span. The company is making money and has great cash flow."

Powerful Minds

The Tax People's Board of Directors reads like a Who's Who of American Business. Among those members is the Chairman of the Board, Mr. James H. Carter, who has an extensive background of business successes.

In 1965, he was the founding president of American Investors Life Insurance Company and served in that position for the first nine years. Today, American Investors is one of the largest life insurance companies in the Midwest.

In 1987, Mr. Carter served as Vice President for TVC Marketing Group of Washington. He developed a large network marketing organization of independent marketing representatives who marketed Pre-paid Legal Services of Ada, Oklahoma. This experience provided Mr. Carter with first-hand knowledge of the networking industry and the people behind the scenes.

Mr. Carter shares the reason he agreed to participate in the growth of The Tax People: "I've known Michael Cooper, and he has served in the network marketing field for decades. When he created the compensation plan for The Tax People's Independent Marketing Associates, he did it with full knowledge of what needed to be improved for the distributors in the field. His goal was to remove the flaws that existed in other companies. That type of thinking drew me toward his good mind."

Mr. Carter continues, "The people in the field must come first, and without question, Michael Cooper has always done that. His extensive experience with other network marketing companies has shown him the negatives and the positives of this industry. Michael has paid his industry dues. The time has come for him to build a company based on his philosophies of the positive aspects of network marketing and placing distributors first.

"Michael is absolutely brilliant with computer knowledge. In today's world, computers and network marketing go hand-in-hand. Computer knowledge is not necessary for distributors, but it is for the people at the helm of a company. Computer genius is required to pay distributors. I don't know of another network marketing company that can keep up to the speed of the daily compensation program that Michael Cooper developed exclusively for The Tax People."

Mr. Carter explains, "Michael's computer knowledge is one of the assets of The Tax People. If you or I started a network marketing company, we'd have to hire a large company and pay top dollar to have a compensation plan developed and programmed into a computer. Each time we needed to write checks, we would have to pay that company on a per check basis. Writing checks would become very expensive. That is what other companies face. They can't afford to write thousands of checks every day. Michael Cooper's genius has made calculating and writing distributor checks extremely affordable and very, very fast."

Mr. Carter confirms, "If Cooper hadn't been brilliant of mind and experienced in network marketing, he could have never put a compensation plan together from concept to computer and made it all come out right. That's the mark of genius. TTP's compensation plan is far and above anything else available in this industry."

It was 1994 when Michael Cooper wrote the software that, for the first time in network marketing history, allowed companies to pay bonuses on a daily basis. The idea had come to Michael several years prior but as he explains, "At that time, even the super computers were not fast enough to track a daily pay plan through thousands of people. The idea had to wait for computer speed to catch up."

Until the power of technology increased, the complex series of calculations performed by computers to write distributors' checks required multiple days. Michael summarizes, "There are only 24-hours in a day. When computers and software required two or three days to calculate and write checks, it was impossible to pay daily."

Mr. Cooper reinforces, "Today, The Tax People is the only network marketing company that can post $1,000,000 worth of sales through 100,000 people in less than four minutes. Our software is worth millions of dollars. Even in the computer world, only a few computer experts are aware that this programming capability exists. Our software and hardware allow us to calculate *daily* bonus checks on a *billion dollars* in sales. We are ready for our inevitable future growth."

The Tax People's computer system has already created distinguished results. Having paid over 100,000 bonus checks and millions-of-dollars to Independent Marketing Associates, the software has calculated every check accurately and on-time.

Mr. James Carter highlights Michael Cooper's abilities: "Whatever it takes, if it's day or night, Michael gets the job done. He has excellent habits. Some people would rather put in four hours and then play golf. Michael's work is his reward — whether with the computers or traveling 1,000 miles for two days of meetings to arrive back home and finish where he'd left off. He has the knowledge, skills and talents to do whatever it takes."

Mr. Carter confides, "You and I could find a few other CEO's who have similar drives. The challenge would be to find the drive plus the skill, talent and compassion. I think that Michael is a one-of-a-kind man when you consider the level to which he cares about people. He does everything possible to benefit all those affiliates with The Tax People.

"As a result, people's future dreams are much greater than ever before. I sit and listen to our Independent Marketing Associates talk about what they have now which they never had before. We have people driving brand new automobiles, living in new homes and earning substantial incomes. It's absolutely a joyful experience to be a part of a company that can create this kind of success for people of all ages."

Upon reflection Mr. Carter states, "With this kind of opportunity, people's potentials are unlimited. At a job, Americans are frozen to a salary for the rest of their lives. No matter how resourceful employees are, their potentials equal their salaries plus small standard-of-living raises. If their salaries are $40,000 a year, with raises they might earn $40,800 next year.

"With The Tax People, if individuals want to enhance their lives, they can make $40,000 *each-and-every month*. As we speak, people of all ages are making that kind of money with their TTP home-based businesses. It is a real turn-on for the people of America to know that they can choose unlimited futures.

"If there is any tribute to be credited to the directors and management of The Tax People, it is providing people of all ages and backgrounds with unlimited futures. The residual incomes created through TTP businesses are among the greatest living assets families can own."

At 72-years-young, Mr. Carter speaks from experience: "People of all ages are having fun doing this business.

Yes, people can make a great deal of money, but there is more. Take all the money in the world and go to some island. You'll find yourself sitting alone. What are you going to do? Is that money helping you if you are alone?"

With a smile Mr. Carter asks, "Now take $10,000 and a bunch of your buddies fishing for a week or whatever you love to do. Are you going to have fun? Darn right. That's what this business can do for you. It's just more fun than I can give thanks for. It really is. I love it.

"This company is an American jewel with an extremely bright future. I just ask people to stay close and aware of it. I can certainly see The Tax People as one of America's largest tax preparation companies."

Doing more than simply watching from the sidelines, Charles Davis, famous for his part in the 1975 and 1976 Super Bowl Championships as a member of the Pittsburgh Steelers, jumped on the opportunity to become a TTP customer. It was May 1998 when a former Chicago Bears player, David Hale, introduced him to TTP's services.

Charles expounds, "Dave sent me an audio by Michael Cooper. I had originally met Michael in 1992. I was impressed with how Michael balanced his genius and communication abilities. Michael is a card-carrying member of Mensa, the genius society. My respect for Michael Cooper is the reason that I took a serious look at The Tax People."

With years of business experience and a degree in marketing from Texas Christian University, Charles is confident when evaluating business opportunities. "The Tax People is a very solid business with strong internal leadership and management. The market is 120,000,000 taxpayers. The tax strategies and advice that TTP has based its services on are directly from the IRS Tax Code and Regulations. TTP is showing people how to use legal information to the benefit of their families.

"A friend of mine always said that if you don't know your rights, you don't have any. TTP is giving people back their legal rights."

The Super Bowl Of Life

Super Bowl winner Earl Christy was a member of the New York Jets and played with Joe Namath when they beat the Baltimore Colts in 1969. The event was considered by some the greatest upset in professional football history. During the game, Earl played defensive back, leading kickoff and punt returner for the Jets.

Earl recently celebrated the 30th anniversary of his television show, *EC Sports Network*, which airs Thursdays and Fridays in Chicago with approximately 1,000,000 viewers.

Active in network marketing, the success Earl has experienced in TTP has been better by comparison than that of any other companies. Earl explains by example, "Everybody who pays taxes needs The Tax People's

56

services. These services truly help families. In return for helping, customers receive compensation. There is no competition compared to other network marketing opportunities or other tax preparation companies."

Earl asserts, "The services of The Tax People are so wanted by individuals that I'm talking to more than just the people I personally know. I can tell anyone about these services and they are interested. I've never had a business opportunity where people are so willing to listen and join. The Tax People is truly an opportunity to express and communicate with people. I'm having great fun with this."

While Earl is having fun helping families put more money back in their pockets, he's also making money himself. "Bonus checks of $1,600 and $2,000 show up in my mailbox. It's phenomenal. Everyone in my organization has seen results and made money. The beautiful part is results and money come quickly. You know what I call TTP? The Super Bowl of Life. Join our team and for the rest of your life you can win by helping others."

The income potential of network marketing has also won the attention of 39-year-old Patrick James, a successful professional seminar leader. Patrick affirms, "In a prior company, my network marketing income was $96,000 a year working about 10 hours a week."

Patrick and his friend Stan Barker were in that prior company together. "So when Stan called me about The Tax People, I listened."

Stan Barker had met with Chris Pulley, a man in his 20's earning over $30,000 a month with his TTP business. Afterwards, Stan contacted Patrick who goes on to tell us, "I was so excited with what Stan told me that I called Delta Airlines and used frequent flyer miles to purchase two first-class, round trip tickets to TTP's home office in Topeka.

"Stan and I are approached about many things. We're rarely interested; but TTP was the first opportunity where they actually pay you just to be involved. Customers are receiving immediate increases in their take-home paychecks just by implementing the strategies. This decision was a no-brainer."

Patrick describes the Topeka meeting where he and Stan met with CEO Michael Cooper and Board Chairman James Carter, "We spent hours drilling them with questions. Then, we attended an evening business meeting where we met one-on-one with Independent Marketing Associates making $25,000 a month. That's all we needed to see.

"Within six hours of returning home, I spoke to three people about The Tax People. They all enrolled. Stan and I held a TTP business meeting with twelve people present. Everyone enrolled and requested another meeting. The next meeting we had 35 people. The following week attendance was over 100."

Patrick describes how TTP has personally helped him: "Between seminars and the stock market, I make a great deal of money. I have set-up corporations and limited partnerships and was sure that I was legally reducing my taxes.

"TTP's tax experts calculated an additional $100,000 in legal deductions that my CPA had missed. That additional $100,000 in write-offs at my 39% tax bracket means I saved $39,000 dollars before I even made a penny with my TTP business!"

Patrick outlines three different types of people who are becoming customers of The Tax People.

"Category number one contains people who like the idea of instant increases in their take-home pay, former IRS agents completing their taxes and complete audit protection.

"Category two comprises people who want to make an extra $400 or $500 a month just to make the family budget stretch.

"Category three involves people who see the huge potential and want to rock-the-house making $50,000 and more a month.

"If all this opportunity did was help people with their taxes, it would be well worth their investment. If they invested $100 a month to put an additional $400 per month back in their pockets, wouldn't it be worth it? Of course it would."

Kent McLaughlin's son Taylor agrees with Patrick and shares the story of life as he knows it with his parents'

TTP business. During grade school classes, Taylor's teacher asked students what they wanted to be when they grew up. Taylor answered, "A networker."

Baffled, the teacher inquired, "What is that?"

Taylor replied, "I don't know, but for the last two years my dad has been a networker. Christmas has been the best ever."

Taylor's father Kent details, "Prior to The Tax People, we had some tough Christmases. Since we've started our TTP business, the income has allowed us to take the kids to the toy store, buy whatever caught their eyes and not worry about the cost. Last year, when we got to the front counter, we had three shopping carts full of toys. We didn't realize how much the kids had until my wife and I spent hours wrapping. Finally, we told the kids that the unwrapped presents were from Santa Claus."

One of the gifts that the McLaughlins are most grateful for is The Tax People opportunity that has developed into their own $1,000,000 annual home-based business.

THE DOOR OPENS
AND LETS
THE FUTURE IN

"The difference between what we do, and what we are capable of doing, would solve most of the world's problems."

— **Gandhi**

Senator Jerry Pierce served in the Oklahoma legislature from 1970 through 1994 before running for Governor, where he finished second in the state Republican primary. After that hard fought and narrowly missed campaign, he continued to serve the state legislature for an additional two years.

It was one of his campaign members who told Senator Pierce about The Tax People as Jerry recalls, "The closest TTP meeting at that time was in Kansas City so I traveled there. I felt comfortable with the services The

Tax People was offering and chose to become a customer. Since then, TTP's *Tax Relief System* has helped my wife Brenda and me keep better records and legally pay less income tax.

"Brenda and I have been business owners for a number of years. I knew The Tax People's *Tax Relief System* was legal. We had been using most of the suggested deductions and strategies all along."

"As time went on, we learned about more deductions that we hadn't used before. We have saved even more money on our taxes. I feel very comfortable sharing The Tax People's services with other families so they can save money on their taxes, too. It was particularly helpful to us in simplifying our record-keeping system and made our tax returns more audit proof."

Senator Pierce comments on government acceptance of The Tax People's tax saving strategies and system: "All we are doing is taking the law and living by it. We are applying the law to our individual lives to develop tax saving strategies.

"The tax-saving concepts and strategies are not new by any means. Rather, TTP is educating taxpayers who may not otherwise know that all of these tax-saving strategies are available to them. TTP has packaged the information in a highly understandable and usable form which can be easily passed from person-to-person, family-to-family."

When Troy Helming first became a customer of TTP, he spoke to both his father and his CPA.

For nine years, Troy owned a successful telephone equipment company. As a businessman, he was immediately impressed with TTP. "I listened to a tape from The Tax People that showed me a few deductions I wasn't taking on my taxes. I sat down with my CPA and reviewed the *Tax Relief System*. He determined the information in the system was correct and that for several years, I had overpaid my taxes. I wasn't mad at my CPA. There were some things that he just didn't know about. I don't expect him to know everything. Since then, I have spoken to several CPA's who are not aware of all of these legal strategies.

"My CPA offered to amend my prior years' returns. I received an additional $7,500 refund for 1995, $6,500 for 1996 and $7,000 for 1997. Just by becoming a customer of The Tax People, I am $21,000 ahead in tax savings and it only cost me $300."

Troy proceeds, "The second person I talked to about The Tax People was my father, a very well known economist, Bill Helming. In 1985 he wrote a tax reform plan called the Helming NCT (National Consumption Tax). In February 1998, the Cato Institute in Washington D.C. used their super computer to evaluate all the proposed alternatives to the current Federal Tax System: flat tax, national retail sales tax, USA tax, VAT and NCT. My father's plan was selected as the number one alternative to our current tax system.

"When Steven S. Moore, Director of the Cato Institute, published the results, Dad received a call from Bill Archer, chairman of the House Ways and Means

Committee. Dad flew out to Washington and has been going out there every two months to testify in front of the Congressional Subcommittee on Tax Reform. Dad's also met with George W. Bush. What I'm saying is that Dad knows a lot about taxes."

When Troy spoke to his father, the very first comment Mr. Helming made about The Tax People was the strength of the business opportunity. Troy talks about his father's comments. "Dad said to his knowledge there was no other company out there on a nationwide scale showing Americans how to legally save on their taxes. He asked me to take the *Tax Relief System* to his own CPA for review. Based on the information in TTP's *Tax Relief System*, the CPA discovered he was missing deductions on my father's taxes."

Troy's father became a customer of The Tax People on the spot.

Next, Troy made appointments with accountants in the U.S. Virgin Islands of St. Thomas, St. John and St. Croix. As U.S. territories, the people of those islands pay federal taxes. Troy discovered that the IRS collects the taxes that the island citizens pay, and then 100% of that money is returned to the local legislature. That local government has been running a deficit and as a result, it keeps people's refund checks for four years. People on the islands don't want to overpay.

Troy signed up 30 people on his first trip. "It is incredible how excited these people are. The average person there is saving about $4,000 a year on their taxes."

Then, Troy spoke to his insurance agent, Adolfo Uriarte, a top producer in Kansas City. According to Troy, Adolfo was paying $9,000 in self-employment tax a year, $14,000 a year in federal income tax and $5,000 for state taxes. This was a total of $28,000 a year in taxes. Troy explains, "He spoke with members of our Tax Dream Team. As a result of their recommendations, Adolfo's annual tax savings was $18,000."[1]

Next, Troy called Harry Singer, a very successful business owner. Singer had been paying his accountant $42,000 per year to take care of his corporate and personal income taxes. As Troy says, "When I asked for a meeting, Harry's secretary told me 'No' 12 times in a row. Finally I got creative. On the thirteenth call, I told the secretary to tell Harry that I could show him how to deduct the cost of private school for his son."

Troy recalls, "Harry answered the phone telling me that I had 30 seconds of his time. I told him that our tax team is a group of former IRS agents and we can guarantee in writing to find him at least $5,000 in new tax deductions.

"Then I told him I would show him how to deduct $5,250 per year per adult child on schooling. He agreed to a 30-minute appointment. While I was at his office we called his accountant who verified our Tax Dream Team's strategies were legal. Harry signed up with The Tax People. Instructing his accountant to use the

---

[1] All figures in this paragraph are rounded.

guidance of The Tax People and the *Tax Relief System*, Harry saved $22,000 on his 1999 taxes."

The deduction for private school tuition is one of the many legal tax strategies utilized by The Tax People as TTP's National Director of Taxes Jesse Cota states, "Structured properly, parents can deduct $5,250 per child for school tuition. There are some limitations that people need to be aware of. The child has to be at least 21 years of age before the parent can take advantage of the deduction. This is a good tax strategy that our clients can use if they plan the right way. We show them how."

Troy was also able to help his friend Kathleen Brock, a ReMax realtor. Kathleen's husband is disabled with a severe health condition. Every quarter they struggled to pay $1,500 in self-employment and other taxes.

Troy continues, "We were able to legally reduce her quarterly payments down to $400. The Tax People put an immediate $1,100 every quarter in her pockets. That helped her cash flow incredibly."

CEO Michael Cooper confirms, "It's not just the Vanderbilt, Kennedy, Walton or Gates families that receive these tax deductions. Every tax deduction that is available to 'the Bill Gates of the world' is also available to every other American taxpayer. People and their accountants must be made aware of those deductions in order to receive them."

Live All You Can

November 1998, the first month Dan and Terri Cook became customers of The Tax People, they received sizable combined take-home pay raises. Dan reveals, "We immediately had $800 additional in our family budget. It changed our lives. Just imagine what an extra $800 every month would do for your family!"

Excitement and relief can be heard in Dan's voice as he says, "My wife Terri, our six kids and I had seriously outgrown the duplex we owned. After six months of building our TTP business, we were able to afford a new home and purchase two new vehicles — all in the same month. Plus, TTP's car program is paying for our new $48,900 Suburban. Our newly discovered tax strategies and the steady daily, weekly and monthly incomes from our TTP business have allowed us to keep our duplex as rental property."

Before TTP, the Cooks were like so many other 40-somethings, putting as much as they could into retirement, knowing they would have to borrow against it for college. Dan continues, "Since starting our TTP business, we know our kids' college tuitions will be paid for without loans."

When the Cooks initiated their TTP business, the hardest information to learn was that without the services of The Tax People, Dan had unknowingly lost a million dollar retirement fund. Dan details, "At 18-years-old, I started building elevators and made extremely good money. If back then, I had applied the *Tax Relief System* and invested my tax savings in mutual funds, that money would have worked itself into a million dollars in the bank. If I had only kept and invested the money that I unknowingly over-paid the IRS! The only way I can live with my mistake is to inform others so they keep their money."

One of the new customers which Dan and Terri introduced to TTP was Dennis Evans who received an instant pay raise of $833.33 per month. Dan explains, "I had asked Dennis 13 times to attend TTP business meetings and each time he stood me up. Finally, he arrived. Halfway through the meeting he leaned over, punched me and asked, 'Why didn't you make me come to the first meeting?'"

Benny and Renee Brown of Amarillo, Texas own a construction company and became customers of The Tax People in October 1997. As Benny recalls, "I've always had my CPA do my taxes. I implemented a few strategies from The Tax People that my CPA hadn't mentioned. The Tax People saved me $6,000. The second year I implemented more TTP strategies and I saved $8,000. That's a total of $14,000 that I would have lost without The Tax People."

Benny cites, "I am not a tax expert; I'm a builder. It's really neat that I don't have to have a mind for taxes but now that I'm a customer, I'm more savvy than before."

The information contained in TTP's *Tax Relief System* guides people to the legal options available to save money.

The Browns were so excited about their $14,000 savings that they began to tell their friends. Benny said, "A good friend of mine has a farming and cattle ranching business. He became a customer. I asked him to send his last 3 years' tax returns into our Tax Dream Team just to see what his accountant was doing and to make sure everything was okay.

"One of The Tax People's professionals called my friend wanting more information. When my friend received the second call from the Tax Dream Team it was to tell him that, for the last three years, he had overpaid his taxes by $43,000 and the IRS was sending it back to him."

Many of the members of the Tax Dream Team are ex-IRS agents who have spent years memorizing the tax code and regulations. As a result, they know how to legally position families and businesses for maximum tax benefit. The Tax People retain tax professionals who are experts in a multitude of business categories such as home-business, agriculture, manufacturing and retail among others.

Benny reveals, "I have another buddy that works at a local feed yard. After he became a customer of The Tax People, he sent them his most recent three years of tax returns. For several years, his wife had a Tupperware business but their CPA would not let them take any home-based business deductions. The CPA told them that it would throw up a red flag for an audit. The Tax Dream Team amended my friend's returns and he's got a $2,700 check on its way."

Donald Alexander, former commissioner of the Internal Revenue Service is quoted saying, "As a citizen, you have an obligation to the country's tax system, but you also have an obligation to yourself to know your rights under the law and possible tax deductions — and to claim every one of them."

Bill Greenfield is an electrical utility manager whose wife, Jeannie, works at JC Penney's. After joining The Tax People, they used a combination of the *Tax Relief System* and personal advice from the Tax Dream Team to save $8,441 on their 1998 tax returns. The Greenfields also received an immediate take-home pay increase of $400 per month.

The Greenfield family had operated a catering business on the weekends that their accountant hadn't taken seriously. As Bill explains, "We had grown tired of paying over $14,000 in taxes each year. I asked my accountant for tax strategies and was told we had no other deductions available to us. You can imagine the accountant's shock when he discovered his advice was half-baked. I knew it wasn't right that Jeannie and I worked so hard and kept so little."

The Greenfields now work their TTP business as a family. Bill explains, "One of our new tax strategies is to pay our teenagers Karlista and Chad $4,250 each for helping us work our business. Really, it's money we would have spent on them anyway, but now it's tax-free for them and 100% deductible for us."

The kids contribute to the family business by answering the phone, taking messages, and putting labels and stamps on post cards and packages.

Bill summarizes, "The kids like our TTP business more than catering. The pay is better and they don't have to do dishes."

Rising Above Reality

Cathy & Kevin Hart became customers of The Tax People in 1997 after a conversation with their neighbor Kent McLaughlin, who was a financial planner and one of the original customers of The Tax People.

Cathy explains, "I operated a daycare from home for five years. I had a wonderful CPA and felt he was giving us every home-based business deduction possible."

One afternoon Cathy was planting new shrubs in her yard. "Kent came over and we started talking. He asked me if I knew that my shrubs were tax deductible. I laughed."

Kent went on to ask Cathy if she was deducting her swing set, washer and dryer, videos and Nintendo. Cathy replied, "My CPA hadn't told me I could."

Kent provided Cathy with a list of legal home-based business deductions. Cathy comments, "I saw several expenses that we were not deducting from our income. I figured if these deductions were real, we had over-paid our taxes $25,000 for the last five years."

Cathy was quite upset but still skeptical. She took the list of deductions to her CPA who told her that all the write-offs on the list were legal. Cathy continues, "I was angry. How could he have let me overpay my taxes all those years? Every year I asked if there was any way to lower our tax bill. Our CPA said we were doing the best we could."

"I told my CPA in order to keep me as a client, he must contact his other clients and tell them he knew how to keep money in their pockets."

Cathy's CPA told her that he didn't specialize in home-based businesses and didn't have time to call his clients. Cathy states, "I told him he was a crook if he didn't do it."

The tax experts at The Tax People amended Cathy and Kevin's past years' tax returns.

Cathy was so excited that she started talking to others. She shares, "I had a friend at church whose family was being forced into bankruptcy. They weren't making enough money to pay their bills. I introduced her and her husband to the tax strategies in the *Tax Relief System*."

"The deductions that The Tax People recommended legally gave my friend's family an extra $400 each month. They were able to apply that to bills and avoided bankruptcy. Within one week of becoming customers, my friend told four people who also became customers. She earned an additional $400 for a total of $800 dollars in less than ten days. It was such a blessing for her that we cried together when her checks came."

Deborah Robards also felt blessed when she became a TTP customer in July 1998. She was the co-owner of a trucking company that had run into financial difficulties. Deborah explains, "Each week we sold company assets in order to put food on our tables. With $7,800 due for insurance and no money in the bank, I was heartbroken when we were forced to close the company."

In Deborah's trucking business she was the last one to get paid, if at all. With her TTP business she receives multiple checks daily, weekly and monthly.

Deborah talks about her success with The Tax People: "In the trucking business every day I was filling out forms and paperwork. Building my TTP business requires only a phone and the ability to dial. I simply tell people I can help them get immediate pay raises on their next paychecks. Every person I talk to on the phone always wants to hear more."

Deborah details the other benefits of her TTP business: "My family used to live from paycheck-to-paycheck, always running out of money before the end of the month. Thanks to TTP, now I run out of *month* before the end of the money. With the additional income I've made from my TTP business, I've been able to have laser surgery on my eyes. I would have never had this surgery without the income from this company. This company has allowed me to buy back my vision."

Deborah has helped many people overcome hard times. "A school janitor was making $1,500 per month and paying $600 for child support and $500 in taxes. Working 40 hours a week this guy was bringing home $400 a month, the equivalent of $2.31 per hour. We increased his take-home pay by $300. This nearly doubled his net income. His wife was a waitress who received an immediate pay raise of $250. The Tax People legally put $550 per month back into that family's pockets."

A smile can be heard in Deborah's voice as she tells of another experience. "A 74-year-old man and his wife became customers of TTP after his mother-in-law was placed in a nursing home. The $3,000 per month for her care was an unexpected expense that crippled the family budget.

"Wanting the best for his wife's mother, this 74-year-old man needed to find a way to supplement his fixed income. At his age, he knew there was little hope of finding a part-time job that would pay enough to cover the nursing home bill. Much to his family's relief, his TTP business is paying for his mother-in-law's care."

Sarah Guetschow is Vice President of The Tax People. Because of her belief in The Tax People services, she enrolled her parents Steve and Gloria Guetschow. The elder Guetschows sold their Wisconsin home causing them to owe a large amount of capital gains tax. They worked with TTP tax expert Tom Steelman. Using his 25-years of IRS experience, the ex-agent turned pro-taxpayer showed the Guetschows how to legally save $18,000 on the property sale.

Amazed with the outcome of the tax savings on the sale, Steve and Gloria asked Mr. Steelman to review the taxes that their previous CPA had completed. Thirty-two year old Sarah explains, "Within 5 minutes of looking over the paperwork and taxes prepared by the other CPA, Tom saw how to get my parents an extra $1,200 back! Dad was just thrilled. It's a great feeling to have helped my parents."

You Reach Your Destination Quicker When You Take Someone With You

Bill & Amanda Fox became TTP customers in October 1998. Bill was involved with a network marketing company and Amanda was an executive assistant at Sprint PCS.

Bill's stepfather, Don Stroh, was one of the first people Bill and Amanda introduced to The Tax People. Don became a customer "just to help the kids out." He already had a high-buck, aggressive CPA who had been completing his taxes for years.

Bill spells out his request to his stepfather: "I asked Don to send his tax paperwork to his CPA and also to The Tax People. I just wanted him to compare."

Don agreed but was confident that his CPA would shine. To Don's surprise, the tax return completed by the CPA showed a $10,000 refund. The return completed by The Tax People computed a refund of over $24,000.

Bill and Amanda felt great about being able to help one of their parents. Next, it was their turn to be helped. Bill tells, "Amanda received a $576.79 per month take-home pay raise. Using the personal guidance of the tax experts at The Tax People, she also received a $3,500 refund at the end of that year. This was the first time she had received a refund in three years!"

Bill relates, "I'm self-employed and thought I knew all the legal deductions available to me. I was surprised when The Tax People saved me $9,100. It was a real eye opener. They also reviewed our last three years' tax returns and discovered in 1995, we'd overpaid. It was great when we opened our mailbox and found a check for $2,500 from the IRS.[2]

"Using the tax advice and strategies available to customers of The Tax People, Amanda and I have saved almost $23,000. How many people that you know who pay taxes want to legally pay less? There is no competition or comparison to the services that The Tax People offer."

Bill confides, "I'm no tax expert. I simply plug individuals into this tax saving system developed by the top tax minds in America. I let the experts show families

---

[2] Figures are rounded.

how to immediately put money back into their pockets every month. You don't need to know about taxes or give any tax advice. I simply tell people about my personal story. Then, I let the Tax Dream Team answer people's tax questions and show them how to save taxes in their situations.

On November 13, 1999 *The Wall Street Journal* reported that "more taxpayers are turning to paid preparers to handle their income tax returns. Based on samplings of returns received through August, 56.2% used paid preparers up from 54.7% in the same period last year."

Based on approximately 120,000,000 personal returns, that's a one year increase of 1,800,000 people turning to the experts. The real question is how many of the experts really know what they are doing?

TTP's Vice President of Sales and Marketing Todd Strand helped bring The Tax People to its inception and serves as the creator of the Tax Dream Team. "As I was talking to tax experts for possible inclusion on our team, I discovered that the more knowledgeable the experts were, the more they realized and admitted that they didn't know everything about taxes.

"It showed me that no *one person* knew all the answers. I determined that we needed a large panel of tax experts with abilities to research tax issues and determine the legal strategies. Plus, they needed to have strong relationships in place with the IRS and other experts.

"Our National Director of Taxes Jesse Cota was formerly with the IRS for 33 years. When he is asked a complex tax question, he calls five or more research specialists who are experts in the particular area in question. This demonstrates how complex taxes really are.

"As a company, I think we are very blessed to have our tax experts. They are the "Who's Who" of the tax world. Individually, other experts may be comparable — united, no one is bigger.

"Prior to TTP, most American families didn't have access to high-powered tax experts. Now they do and we provide more than just expertise. We make it possible for all people to *apply* that expert knowledge. Before we began to offer our services, families were only *talking* about tax deductions. Now, they are *taking* them. The result is money. People are paying fewer taxes and receiving larger refund checks. We produce the results — safely and legally."

Dave Robins and his family started using the services of The Tax People in February 1998. He recalls, "The first year my family used TTP's *Tax Relief System* we were shocked when we saved almost $10,000 on our taxes. Prior to TTP, I was a financial planner. I thought that I knew every tax strategy there was for operating a business from home.

"When I became involved with TTP, it was staggering to learn of all the deductions that I had been missing, like how to pay my kids tax-free, write-off even more meals or entertainment and make our vacations tax deductible."

Like most financial planners, Dave was looking for a way to show clients how to free up money in their budgets so they could invest more in their futures. "I immediately realized TTP's *Tax Relief System* and tax services would show families how to realize $400-$800 or more each month in tax savings. Using this service, I showed clients with 30-year mortgages how to pay off their loans in six to seven years without having to earn any new money. Instead, they used the money that they had previously been paying the IRS and apply it to the principal on their home mortgages each month."

Dave continues, "I showed my clients how they could invest their tax savings and double the principal in six years or less. That's without adding any more money to their accounts. Most people become customers of TTP on the spot."

Dave's belief in The Tax People was so high that he placed his whole life on hold to inform others about the tax saving benefits. He asked his wife and four children to support his decision. In doing so, Dave knew it would change his family's entire financial future for the better. Due to the commitment of the entire family, Dave's TTP business grew quickly.

Dave recounts, "For the first three months of my TTP business, I kept selling insurance and mutual funds. The Tax People business became so successful that it just took over. There was and still is no competition. I am not a marketing genius, but I am smart enough to see when a product or service is rock solid, comprehensive and solves a problem for masses of people.

"Within six months, I was close to achieving the company ranking of Diamond. That would increase my monthly business income because I'd be sharing in a percentage of the company's total residual monthly revenues."

The marketing expenses of building a business so quickly caught up and Dave found himself temporarily over-extended. He needed money. "I was told to call Michael Cooper for help. I was hesitant to call him for a loan. Michael hadn't known me for long; we had met only a few months prior. My situation forced me to make the call. Michael simply asked how much I needed and if I wanted it sent overnight. I had a hard time believing it! I now know first-hand that Michael really cares and goes the extra mile for people."

Dave's business went on to earn the much-desired Diamond status and he gratefully repaid the loan. "When I first joined TTP, I had computed that a person who achieved Diamond status could earn a minimum of a mid-to-high six figure income. Was I ever glad to find out that I was right! Today, my family and I are enjoying the financial security and freedom of our Diamond lifestyle."

KNOW YOUR LIMITS, THEN IGNORE THEM

"If you risk nothing, then you risk everything."
— **Geena Davis**, Actress

Philippine-American Arlene Agoncillo describes her cash crunch when she first became a TTP customer: "My husband Adolfo and I were broke, barely living paycheck-to-paycheck, raising four children from 1-year-old to 15. We couldn't afford to have me work and pay for daycare. We needed to do something because we couldn't make ends meet on one salary."

The Agoncillos were faced with the same challenge that plagues many American families — availability of affordable, yet safe, daycare. A national study cited that the annual cost of full-time daycare is about $7,500 per child. This means a family's second income earner could need to make as much as $30,000 a year to pay daycare costs alone.

Arlene describes their situation: "When we were introduced to The Tax People, we were already two months behind on our mortgage payments. We were in bad shape financially. I remember every day looking at my children and wondering how we were going to live."

Arlene and Adolfo made a choice. "Desperate, we took a chance and used money from our third late mortgage payment to start our TTP business. Within one week, we were able to recoup our entire investment and pay one of our late mortgage payments. Two weeks later, we had earned enough money to pay our other two late payments bringing our mortgage current."

"Seven months into our TTP business, the checks keep coming. We have earned up to $3,000 in just one day. We average about $3,000 a week. Now we're making double house payments and will soon have our home paid off."

Arlene pauses as she quietly reflects, "I never again want to feel the pain of wondering if my children will be homeless."

As mementos, Arlene makes copies of their TTP checks. She explains, "After only seven months, we have a six-inch, three-ring binder full of check copies. We're starting to fill the next binder. Every day we receive checks for $300, $600 and $900, sometimes up to six checks a day."

"It feels good not to be hurting for money, but success is not just the money; it's when we help other people out of troubled times. Being so close to losing everything, we know how painful it is for other people. We have developed many friendships by just caring."

Not all people start as determined as Arlene & Adolfo; but eventually, they end up there. Lito Villamayor was very skeptical and cautious when he received a call from a friend about The Tax People's services: "After I received the information, the first person I called was my accountant. She reviewed it and told me the tax-saving strategies TTP recommended were reasonable and legal."

Lito continues, "With my accountant's blessing, I became a TTP customer. TTP has been very, very good for me. After six months, my income averages over $5,000 each month. I've had prior successes in network marketing but have never seen one like this.

"Success comes easily when offering services that people want. Customers want to remain involved because they are receiving immediate increases in their take-home pay and earning bonus checks from their TTP businesses. In other network marketing companies, less than 10% of the people stay to build businesses. In The Tax People, I have personally introduced 19 customers. All of them are still actively building their businesses after several months. Many are choosing early retirement from their jobs because their TTP businesses are replacing their employment incomes."

Bill & Amanda Fox replaced their other sources of income with earnings from the TTP business that the couple started in October 1998. At the time, Bill was operating a network marketing business that offered pre-paid legal services.

"Before joining The Tax People, in my other network marketing company, the most money I earned in one month was $4,000. I struggled and was disappointed because usually it was closer to $2,000 a month."

Then the couple joined The Tax People. Bill explains, "It was so much easier to make money in TTP. Our third month we made $5,500. Two months later, we were earning $10,000 a month by using a VCR and television to show people a 20-minute video. It explained how The Tax People guaranteed new customers an additional $5,000 in legal tax deductions or they would return every penny of the customers' money."

Before And After Tax Savings

American taxpayers number 120,000,000 and in 1998 alone paid a sizable portion of the $2,700,000,000,000 in taxes collected that year. (Yes, that is $2.7 *trillion* from the pockets of families just like yours!) The national watchdog group, The Tax Foundation, has documented that 1998 tax collections increased a shocking 58.4% over the amount collected in 1990.

Childhood friends turned business partners, Kent McLaughlin, Tom Silvio and Mike Accurso decided to reverse that trend. In doing so, they experienced pleasant results for both themselves and their clients.

First, by offering the services of The Tax People the trio turned a near-bankrupt financial planning firm into a business empire earning an income of over five-digits each month.

Second, and most importantly, they began making immediate and positive impacts on their clients' lives. Tom explains, "Our clients depended on us, as financial planners, to show them how to meet their financial goals. We knew exactly how to invest for retirements, buy new homes and save for their kids' college costs. Our clients were thrilled right up to the point of parting with the money. Even if it was only $100, families couldn't swing it. Our only options were to advise our clients to cut their spending or work a second-job. Neither was appealing."

Kent interjects, "Then we saw that The Tax People offered a service that legally and immediately increases families' take-home pay. We realized our clients had another option. By legally reducing their taxes, they could save money for colleges, retirements and homes without having to get a second job or curb their lifestyles."

Kent, Tom and Mike used their newly discovered knowledge as rocket fuel for success. Tom explains that they focused their combined energies towards one target: "Many middle-class families are overpaying their taxes by $10,000 and more a year. They are handing their retirements, future homes and children's' college funds over to the IRS. Without money, many families are ripped apart."

Mike summarizes, "We just wanted to repair the financial pains and pressures that families were struggling with. The gap between the rich and poor was growing. Legally minimizing the amount of taxes paid puts more money back into families' pockets and closes the gap. Middle and lower-income families instantly have more money to spend, invest and retire. This strategy allows American families to cash in, slow down and live better."

The results of a 1998 survey conducted by Roper Starch show that 43 percent of Americans place "to be independent of others" at the top of their financial goals. The survey results also reveal that self-employed individuals rate their daily work 15 percent more satisfying than their corporate counterparts. The self-employed surveyed also were more positive about their job security than employees of established companies.

Freedom, Freedom, Freedom

Ryan Vanderpool describes himself as "an average car guy trying to make a living" who understands the stress of trying to make ends meet. As the manager of an automotive fleet sales and leasing department for seven years, Ryan had been competing in a low-ball market selling large volumes of cars to a finite number of corporate clients.

He explains, "I strained to succeed in a cutthroat industry, 60 to 70 hours per week, plus I commuted 12 hours a week, in order to provide for my family. I made a nice 6-figure income, but the company owned me."

Lacking the freedom to enjoy his prosperity, Ryan says, "I would come home, spend an hour with my family and then go to sleep. I'd wake the next morning, get ready and go to work to do the same thing every day. I'd have off work every other weekend to be with my family. Instead, I'd sleep trying to recharge myself for Monday."

Trying to find freedom, Ryan had been involved in network marketing in the 1990's. "I knew network marketing had merit. I knew people could make great money, but I tried network marketing twice and failed miserably both times. I figured it wasn't for me."

"The Tax People business is different from the other home-based opportunities I've seen or tried," Ryan comments. Only nine months into his TTP business, Ryan replaced his six-figure income as an employee of the auto dealership. During 2000, Ryan's income is on target to exceed $50,000 a month. That's $600,000 a year — just 24-months after starting his TTP business.

Ryan talks about what initially attracted him to TTP: "Whether people failed or succeeded, they put an immediate $400 and more back into their pockets every month. This money was legally redirected from paying taxes to paying credit cards."

Ryan continues, "That's significant because statistics report that Americans filed 1.4 million bankruptcies last year. Eighty-percent could have been avoided with an extra $300 a month.

"Bankruptcy is often not lack of money; it's lack of *knowledge*. Most families facing financial difficulties have the extra money; they just don't realize it. They are overpaying their taxes, supporting the government instead of supporting their families."

Saving America
One Family At A Time

American's leading tax strategist, Jeff Schnepper, is also author of the much recommended book *How To Pay Zero Taxes* (17th edition, McGraw-Hill). In his book, he quotes what The Tax Foundation study concluded:

- A family earning $25,000 annually would pay 32 percent of its income in taxes;

- A family making $50,000 per year would owe 36.6 percent to federal, state and local governments;

- A family earning $100,000 each year would pay 41.5 percent of that income in taxes; and

- A family making $200,000 would owe taxes of 44.5 percent.

The *KARE-11 Evening News* in Minneapolis reported that according to The Tax Foundation, the average

American family is spending more on taxes than they are on food, housing and clothing combined.

The watchdog organization, Americans for Tax Reform, reports that employees work until July 3rd, six months of each year, to earn enough money to pay all their taxes.

Apply that fact to an *USA Today* finding that reports the American family's mean income is $38,900. A family earning $38,900 would spend around $12,448 on taxes leaving only $2,204 a month to live on. How many families do you know who could eat, buy clothing and pay their mortgages and bills on $2,204 a month without straining? It's easy to see how overpaying taxes is forcing many American families into bankruptcy.

Ryan spells out what he's doing to help: "People want information on how to legally reduce their taxes and immediately increase their take-home pay without asking for raises. Once I started telling people that I knew about an organization which could show them how to do that, they listened."

Ryan reasons, "Owners of TTP businesses can earn substantial residual incomes by jumping on the most solid financial trend in decades — using legitimate home-based businesses to legally reduce taxes. Unlike other tax reduction techniques, TTP home-based businesses actually create large streams of income in addition to tax savings."

Kathy Coover is enjoying the tax savings of her home-based enterprise. "I became a TTP customer hoping to legally lower my taxes. I didn't realize how much The Tax People would help me. After reviewing their *Tax Relief System*, I fell off my chair when I realized that I had overpaid my taxes by $30,000 for the last 5 years. Neither my CPA nor the IRS stopped me from overpaying. I reflected on how many people I knew in the same rut, not knowing they have simple, legal options to keep their money."

Now Kathy is telling others about The Tax People and enjoying the financial rewards of her home-based business. "By my third month in The Tax People, I was earning $7,700. By my ninth month, my income was $20,000 per month. At this growth rate, I should be making $40,000 a month by my 15th month in business. I'm not a tax expert. I simply introduce new customers who use The Tax People's customized, hands-on expertise to attain powerful results."

Kathy has personally introduced 50 new customers. The key to her success is that those people have introduced other customers. She talks about her organization's growth: "Once people receive their instant pay raises or their tax problems are resolved, they want to help others. In nine months, my business grew from zero to 1,850 people. People are making the kind of incomes they deserve. Right away, they are making great money and saving on their taxes. People are very happy and, as a result, are building their businesses."

"During the first month of my TTP business, I realized it was going to grow fast. I had so many people interested, becoming customers and telling their friends who do the same. I have been the top money earner in several network marketing companies but have never experienced that kind of network marketing growth happen so quickly.

"When I introduce new customers, I simply follow up to make sure newcomers have participated in the conference calls with TTP's Tax Dream Team for step-by-step directions and have used that information to receive immediate pay raises. It's much easier calling people to congratulate them on their pay raises than calling to see if vitamins are making them feel better or soap is getting their clothes cleaner."

Kathy explains how she approaches people about TTP services: "I say, 'If I could show you how to reduce your taxes and receive an instant pay raise, would you like to hear about it?' For every 10 people I ask, nine of them are interested. Increasing take-home pay and reducing taxes are hot subjects. People are tired of paying all those taxes and are looking for legal ways to reduce their burdens."

Kathy's busy schedule starts at 8:00 a.m. "I'm working the business 12 hours a day right now. Some days, like Friday afternoons, I take off. I know by working like this for two years, after that, I'll be able to kick back and enjoy. Even with my busy schedule, I still enjoy flexibility and freedom. I can pick and choose my hours.

I always have the time to be 'Mom' and attend my son Erik's golf tournaments."

Erik, 12, works with his mother in the family business. Kathy pays him $4,250 that is tax-free to Erik and tax deductible for Kathy. "Erik works the computer, makes deposits and takes care of the mail. Our TTP business is teaching him good work ethics. The money Erik earns goes toward his golf. He is an excellent tournament player."

Thrilled that she is able to provide for herself and her son, Kathy summarizes, "The Tax People is a service that helps families keep more of their money. Plus, for those who want to earn money from home, the business opportunity offers sizable income. I feel building my TTP home-based business is a wise investment of time.

"Our corporate parent, TTP, is solid and headed for a billion dollars in revenue. Through the compensation plan, each customer can receive a portion of that gross income. If people want to be involved with a caring, solid, well-financed and growing company with credible leadership, they should become customers of The Tax People."

Serving A Starving Crowd

The Tax People is the world's fastest growing tax service company and one of the few companies worldwide with the potential to achieve the status of a billion-dollar company in only 6 years.

The corporation has reported a 1200% monthly gross income increase over a 22-month period. Back in January, 1998 the company had gross revenues of $250,000 per month with 2,000 customers. For the month of November, 1999 TTP reported 20,000 customers resulting in gross revenues of $3,000,000.[1]

CEO Michael Cooper explains his philosophy behind a compensation plan that ensures Independent Marketing Associates share in TTP's revenue: "The problem with most network marketing compensation plans is that they pay only a certain number of levels from your original position.

"Could you imagine owning a McDonald's where you are paid only for the first six customers who order breakfast in the morning? Would you continue to flip burgers and let corporate McDonald's keep all the rest of the money from all your other customers? Of course not. Imagine owning a shoe store where on the first six people you made a profit but on the rest of them you didn't. You'd fail as a business.

"In other network marketing companies, as your organization grows, you may eventually have tens of thousands of people the company won't pay you for. The company earns money from every person in your organization, but *you* don't. In other compensation plans, you'd be lucky to receive payment on 5% to 10% of the total number of people in your organization.

---

[1] Figures are rounded.

"When I was a network marketing distributor in a telecommunications company, I had built a downline of 28,000 people.[1] I was paid on the sales volume of only 2,400 of those people. The company was earning money on the balance of my other 25,600 clients and not paying me a cent because those clients were outside my 'pay zone.' There's something philosophically wrong with that.

"If you owned a shoe store or a McDonald's, you would expect to earn money from every business sale. If you own a network marketing business, you should expect and receive the same.

"We pay multiple bonuses on every sale in our organization, through infinity. If a sale is made somewhere by someone in your organization, our Trilogy Bonus will make sure you get paid."

Michael details a brilliantly simple illustration of how he can assure all TTP Independent Marketing Associates (IMA's) are paid on every business sale in their organizations: "Presume you own a McDonald's with three cash registers where people line up to order. You're busy all day long. At the end of the day, on each cash register you hit buttons and total your sales. That's what every cash register in America does.

"In our software, you have three cash registers. Each register captures the sales of an organization of customers called your success-line. These three organizations are comprised of people you have introduced to our services, their customers and their customers to infinity. Whether it's the first customer or the fifteen-thousandth customer, our software cash registers will capture the volume in your organization.

"At the end of each day, we total the number of sales in your cash registers. When three sales have occurred at each of your three registers, we pay you $300. When 6 sales occur at each of your three registers, you receive $600. When 9 sales occur at each register, you receive $900. We call this our Trilogy bonus."

In addition to the Trilogy bonus checks that are totaled and sent daily, IMA's can qualify for a free car. It is paid for by The Tax People but selected and owned by the Independent Marketing Associate.

Michael explains, "With only 18 personal sales, our IMA's qualify for the car program. We've had people qualify for their free car in less than two weeks. Less than two weeks in our business and they can buy a Lexus, Mercedes, Viper, Suburban or whatever their dream vehicle is — and we pay for it."

TTP Independent Marketing Associates can earn multiple bonuses including a monthly sharing of over 10% of the company's total residual revenues. Michael details, "One such pool is specifically designed for new IMA's to share a percentage of the total residual income generated by the company, existing IMA's and 'big hitters.' It allows fairly new producers to earn sizable money quickly."

Michael continues, "Imagine if Bill Gates gave $100 billion dollars to the people who helped him build Microsoft. He could create 100,000 millionaire families and, yet, would still be one of the richest men in the world."

Michael concludes, "I don't want to be one of the richest men due to counting money; I want to be one of the richest men when counting the number of families I've helped transform, the number of parents that I've been able to help get back to their kids."

Family First

For 35 years, family expert Eileen Galinsky, author of the book *Ask The Children*, has studied the work vs. family dilemma. As founder and president of the Families and Work Institute in Manhattan, she set out to determine what kids think about their working parents. To discover the answer, Ms. Galinsky surveyed 1,023 children nationwide, as well as 605 mothers and fathers.

The results indicated that kids are fine with parents working. Young people just want their folks to be less tired, distracted and irritable when they arrive home. Kids want their parents around when it matters most — school plays, ball games and when they are stuck at home with the flu.

In a December, 1999 *People Magazine* article, Ms. Galinsky revealed, "Adults have misunderstood the real problem — it isn't just that they work but how they work — and how that affects their parenting."

One of Ms. Galinsky's most unexpected findings was that two-thirds of the 8 to 18-year-olds surveyed said they worry a great deal about their parents. One teen told of worrying that one of her parents would get sick and wondering what would happen to her family. A real concern for two-earner households was that both incomes are already stretched.

People Magazine also quotes Ms. Galinsky: "Overwhelmingly, kids — especially from families struggling economically — see money as a way to pay taxes and bills and reduce the stress their parents are under. This is not about greed. Kids say their parents' stress interrupts the time and energy they have to focus on the children. Specifically I heard, 'They complain if I say the least little thing. I get my head taken off.'"

When Ms. Galinsky surveyed a group of high school students about what they would remember most about their teen years, they repeatedly described small moments. One girl talked about her mother, who walked alongside her when she competed at swim meets and encouraged her.

The answers from Ms. Galinsky's survey prove the importance of families having opportunities to earn good money and have time freedom by work from home.

A recent *Work Trends Survey*, conducted in partnership by Rutgers University and the University of Connecticut, confirms an American paradox. While 82% of adults surveyed have the emotional desire to prioritize their families first, their financial concerns result in different realities.

When given the option between earning more money or working fewer hours at their current jobs, finances forced 58% to neglect their families and select earning more money.

People who start TTP home-based businesses no longer have to choose between their families and their incomes. Earning in excess of $30,000 a month with their TTP business, Janet and Steven Hutchinson are among many parents who have discovered this truth. Janet explains, "Steven and I used to think that our choice was between being at home with our children on a day-to-day basis or earning a substantial income. The beautiful thing we discovered is that families can have both.

"Now that we know this, Steven and I would live in a refrigerator box before we would compromise time with our kids. That is our bottom line. Whether your challenge is a J-O-B that limits you from your family or your children who monopolize your time, your challenge should be the very reason you build a TTP business.

"If you want the reality of having absolute time freedom and the opportunity to earn unlimited wealth, then owning a TTP business is for you."

Janet describes her days: "If you were to come to my house and watch me build this business you would see a woman without make-up wearing tattered jeans, a sports bra and a headset chasing her kids. It is not a pretty picture. I dread the day when there are monitors where you can view the people you are speaking to.

"With four kids ranging from 7 months to 17 years, my mornings start early. I call people first thing. Then I bring business to a halt, feed the kids and send the older ones off to school. Next, more phone time with the Independent Marketing Associates in my organization. Then, Steve and I strap the babies in and go for a walk to clear our heads and spend quality time with the kids. For the rest of the day Steve and I rotate between which of us has our hands on the babies. Whoever is not focused on our children is the one promoting the business at that moment."

The Families and Work Institute in New York City conducted a survey that revealed that 75 percent of mothers considered the daycare arrangements that they depend on to care for their children to be second-rate. Of the two-income families with pre-schoolers, 66 percent would rather care for their own children — if they only had the money to keep one parent at home.

According to *Network Marketing Lifestyles* magazine, only four percent of American companies provide reimbursement of child care costs when employees work late. Only six percent of employers do so when their employees travel for business; six percent provide child care for school-age children on vacation and only four percent provide back up for employees when their regular child care plans unexpectedly fall through.

Certainly a strong argument for working at home. The Hutchinsons agreed and started their TTP business out of the love and concern for their four children: Rachel, 17, Rebekah, 14, Gwyneth, 2, and Greyson, 7 months. Jane explains, "They motivate us every morning to get up, get out and do this business. Steve and I share the goal.

"There is nothing that we want to deny our children because we don't have the financial ability to provide it for them. That's not to say that we don't teach our children to work toward their own dreams. We revel in the idea of providing what they need to go after their dreams."

Janet knows, "It is important that my girls realize they can capture their financial dreams. I was raised believing women didn't belong in the work place. I saw myself as having incredible potential, but I feared going after it. When I worked for others, I was aware that my employers were making most of the money. Building our TTP business has really helped me learn my potential and grow into greatness."

Janet sums up her experience: "A short time into working other networking companies, most people find something about the opportunities that makes them sick to their stomachs. Not with The Tax People. We've been customers of TTP since November 1998 and the more we know, the more we love it. The closer you look, the better we look."

Part-Time Efforts
Full-Time Results

Eighteen months into his TTP business, Tom Kehne loves the way it looks and feels. Tom is a pilot for the Department of Treasury, United States Customs Service. He explains his choice to start his part-time TTP business: "I am a conservative person. I've never wanted anything to do with network marketing; but I've always wanted a home-based business. I couldn't find anything that matched my personality. I don't want to sell soap or change people's buying habits. The Tax People was exactly the home-based business that I was looking for."

"I've been working my TTP business part-time for 18 months. My annual residual income from my part-time, home-based business is $50,000[2] and growing at about 15% every month. This business allowed me to create substantial revenues in a short period of time and still keep my full-time job. As a professional pilot, I earn over $100,000 a year, have a benefits package most people dream of and 13 years vested towards a sizable pension. Even though my TTP business will replace my income as a pilot, I like flying and want to continue. It's great to have the financial cushion TTP has provided."

Tom's TTP business provides him perks in addition to substantial income. "Using The Tax People strategies, I legally saved $11,000[2] in taxes my first year. Then, June 1999 I bought a motor home. My family and I spent the summer months enjoying a 7,200 mile road trip across

---

[2] Figure is rounded.

America. On our travels, I introduced four new customers and was able to write off the whole trip.

"What other type of business would allow you to deduct family vacations? Just let people know you can show them a system to legally reduce their taxes, get their business cards and you are set."

Tom talks about an upcoming decision: "I love my job as a pilot. But, what will I do when the alarm goes off at 7 a.m., I'm earning $250,000 a year in my TTP business and I don't feel like getting up? If I'm faced with a dilemma, that's a good one to have."

People Say "Yes"

Rhonda Browning is The Tax People's corporate Support Manager for its Independent Marketing Associates. She explains, "People who have never considered network marketing before are now becoming customers. Then they see our *Tax Relief System* along with the tax savings and income results others are experiencing. They can't help but become customers."

Rhonda proceeds, "The next question is always, 'Why didn't someone think of this before?' People are amazed Americans have paid taxes for decades before someone developed and offered this type of service.

"The first to grab people's attention is significant, legal tax savings. Next, they see the income opportunity. The topper is the retro-active and current audit protection from our Tax Dream Team. People realize that America's most powerful team of tax professionals protects them. Our IMA's don't *sell* TTP services. They simply talk about the results individuals are achieving and people want to become customers."

Debbie Goroza listened and acted when she heard about The Tax People's services. Having survived a past audit before becoming a TTP customer, she was comforted by The Tax People's audit protection. But the tax savings and additional income changed her life. "I started my TTP business September 1999 on a part-time basis. I was shocked when I earned $2,000 my first month! My second month, I earned $2500. Then, I saved $5,000 on my taxes. In just two months, I put an additional $9,500 back into my family's budget."

Debbie explains, "People who don't learn how to take the available, legal deductions will continue to overpay their taxes. I used to be one of them."

"Since becoming a customer of The Tax People and having access to current and retroactive audit protection, I sleep better at night. I don't fear the IRS. If I am audited in the future, TTP's Tax Dream Team will handle it for me. I wouldn't even have to talk to the IRS. When I deduct an expense according to TTP's *Tax Relief System* and *if* the IRS made an adjustment, I would only pay the tax. The Tax People would pay the penalties and interest. That makes saving money on taxes comfortable and safe."

More Than Just Surviving, They're Succeeding

Before learning about The Tax People, Preston and Jane Blair had struggled for over a decade in an attempt to survive major tax problems. Jane explains, "We know what it's like to look over your shoulder in fear of what the IRS is going to do next. Our credit was destroyed. Even though as business owners we earned significant money, we couldn't secure a car loan, a business loan or get a credit card."

Jane reveals, "We were trapped for 13 years and almost immediately The Tax People freed us.

"As we talk to people about TTP, we are finding many families in the same situation. We had no idea other families were hurting like ours. When you looked at our family, you would have had no idea that we had such difficult problems with the IRS."

Since their release from the clutches of the IRS, the couple has decided to help other families find freedom and immediate pay raises. As a result, nine months into their TTP business, Preston and Jane Blair are already earning over $10,000 per month. Within 18 months, the couple believes they will be earning over $100,000 a month.

Jane asserts: "The Tax People is all the good of network marketing without the bad. Tax People Independent Marketing Associates don't have to change anyone's buying habits. As a result, we can build organizations very quickly. We talk to people and they sign up the same day. People watch the company video at the TTP Web site and sign up immediately.

"It's easy to talk to people about immediate pay raises, saving money on taxes and solving IRS problems. Every American wants to sleep comfortably at night knowing that they are protected. They want more-than-enough money in their bank accounts and want the guarantee the cash will be there in the morning."

Money Provides More Than Hope

Prior to becoming a customer of The Tax People, Larry Dismond was Mayor of Harlem, New York for 20 years. He retired to Las Vegas where the International Council of Mayors appointed him Community Mayor. In this volunteer position, Mr. Dismond heads-up community efforts to help over 12,000 blind and handicapped children in the Las Vegas area.

Larry encapsulates his experiences: "My heart goes out to the families who suffer all the way from Harlem to Vegas, families burdened by finances. I've seen the lack of money destroy families, break homes and starve children. I've seen these problems relieved by lifting tax burdens and providing families with the newly found incomes. That's why I believe so strongly in the services of The Tax People."

Parents of four girls, Rita Bohol and her husband scratched a living from Hawaii's tourism industry. The

Bohols realized they were trading time with their children for money. Feeling their lack of money was wearing her family thin, Rita decided financial repair was in order. "My husband and I have found a way to stop scrambling for money. By starting our TTP business, we were able to increase our paychecks by over $400 a month. Above our pay raises, within our first 10 days, we earned $1,800. We're looking forward to being debt-free within six months.

"Within a year, I believe our TTP business will grow to replace my income and allow me to work from home. My daughters are entering their teen years. Being at home with my family to take care of them, help them with homework and guide them will enhance our family dramatically."

FOR FAST-ACTING RELIEF TRY SLOWING DOWN

"When people go to work, they shouldn't have to leave their hearts at home."
— **Betty Bender**

The word is getting out about the secret lives of employees.

It's the middle of the afternoon. An executive leaves his office with the computer humming on his desk and his suit coat hanging on his chair. He calmly walks past the company's front reception desk with cigarette in hand. It appears that he's headed out for a smoke.

Walking into the elevator he pushes "b" for basement rather than "1" for ground level. As the doors reopen, he steps into the parking garage and jumps into his car. His calm appearance melts and a cold, nervous sweat comes over him as he sneaks out of the garage and races away. What's happening? Has this "company man" gone mad?

No. He's just learned that his kids are stranded at school. But he can't tell his fellow employees that he's left for something so — personal. He hopes they'll just lose track of him or think he disappeared into another meeting.

The Ford Foundation completed a major study called *Relinking Life and Work*. This document reveals people's trepidation of placing their families first for fear of becoming expendable. "Some people give false reasons for leaving work early. Some secretly take children on business trips. Others leave their computers on while picking up children from sporting events, hoping to return to work before they are discovered."

Most employees are paying the ultimate price as Amber and Bob Schaffer discovered.

It was Bob who enrolled the couple as TTP customers. Amber talks about her experience: "I never thought network marketing would be my ticket to retirement from 11 years as a heavy equipment operator, but it has been. In addition, it has made my family more money than we have ever had. It was my husband Bob who had the entrepreneurial mindset and found a way to make us a family again."

She states, "The construction industry was taking its toll on me. I'm 5'5" and about 110 pounds and had been working 70 to 80 hours every week running heavy highway construction equipment. On top of that I was spending 12 to15 hours per week traveling to the job site. There were many weeks where I was home only long enough to sleep, wake, shower and leave again. I had no life and little, if any, family time.

"I felt guilty that I was gone all the time and not being Mom for Lindsey, our 16-year-old, and Jimmy, who is 11. Lindsey was 5-years-old when I started working construction. Bob played Mr. Mom to our kids while operating his window installation business from our home with 9 employees and also marketing cruise trips in the evening."

The Schaffer's price for prosperity was high. "We were making over $240,000 a year but it was nearly killing us. Over 35% of our income went to taxes. When we started our TTP home-based business, the Tax Dream Team showed me how to adjust my W-4, pay fewer taxes and receive an immediate pay raise of $1,000 per month. The first year — using the *Tax Relief System* and even after decreasing the taxes we paid each month by $1,000 per month — we still received an additional $12,700 REFUND! That shocked us since normally we paid the IRS that extra $1,000 a month plus at least $3,500 more at the end of the year. This was a HUGE tax saving for us. It changed our LIVES."

The Schaffers now have a new source of income that has also brought their family back together. Amber continues, "Because we earn over $20,000 a month in our home-based TTP business, we've been able to replace our other incomes. Our TTP income keeps growing. Bob has sold his window installation business and has stopped selling cruises. I've retired from construction and became the full-time mom I always wanted to be."

Amber continues, "People ask us, 'Being so strapped for time, how did you do it?'"

"For a good three months, we talked to people every day about TTP. We got on the phone every night and called people. Just 20 months into the business and we have over 6,000 individuals in our organization. We personally sponsored 35 of those people."

Talking about her new life Amber says, "Life is so different now. We get up when we're finished sleeping. We spend money any time. We go anywhere, any time. I never liked having a boss who told me when I could go on vacation, what kind of car I could afford or if I was going to get a pay raise. Now, Bob and I have time freedom and an uncapped income. Best of all, now I'm my own boss!"

Corporate Business Expert Endorses Home-Based Business

In an April 1999 interview in *Network Marketing Lifestyles* magazine, popular business icon Stephen Covey endorsed network marketing as a way of life. His book *The Seven Habits of Highly Effective People* has been on *The New York Time's* bestseller list for more than 10 years selling over 5 million copies.

A quote from Covey reads, "I think network marketing has come of age."

It is Covey who has come of age — at least enough to understand the power of network marketing. Continuing, Covey confirms, "It's become undeniable that it's a viable way to entrepreneurship and independence for millions of people."

Later in the interview, Covey was asked, "Why do you think they (people) go into this business, as opposed to another kind?" Covey replied, "Network marketing offers them more freedom. You can say, 'Now, when are my kids' events? I don't want to miss them. I'm going to at least 80 percent of them.' Or, 'When am I going to be able to spend more time with my spouse? Why not organize and set that up?' You have more freedom and control over your life."

Home-Based Business Includes Family Fun

Frank and Pam Leonard can tell you about the freedom and control that their TTP business provides their family. "Our kids attend school year round and have off during the months of February, June and October. By June 1999, the tenth month in our TTP business, everything was going great. The kids were off school so we decided to celebrate by renting a cabin for a weekend and invited the families in our TTP organization."

The Leonard family embraces their new lifestyle as Pam shares, "When we arrived home from the cabin, it was time to attend a TTP regional convention in Las Vegas for four days at the Luxor Hotel. Another family vacation became a tax deductible business trip.

"From Vegas, Tara and J.C. went to visit their grandparents in Arizona. Frank and I hit the road for another business trip. On the way home, we picked up the kids, rented a large RV and drove cross-country to Michael Cooper's house for a 4th of July party. There were plenty of other kids at the Coopers for Tara and J.C. to make friends with while riding horses and all-terrain vehicles on Michael's 100-acre ranch. It was awesome.

"By the time we made it home to California, a month had passed and the kids had to start school the next day.

"At school, J.C. handed out TTP packets and told his teachers and other kids that they have to cut their taxes. Tara enrolled Rick and Lisa Lavado, the parents of her friend Corey. Tara spent the night at their house telling them about The Tax People and how it changed our lives.

"A few Saturdays ago we met one of the Independent Marketing Representatives in our organization for breakfast. Tax deductible. Then the kids, Frank and I went to the new mall and had fun buying clothes. The kids spent their own tax-free earnings. Next, we attended a business presentation and dinner out that evening. Again, tax deductible. This lifestyle allows us to operate our business, earn our income, save on taxes and enjoy a close-knit family.

"All of these same activities we used to engage in after tax and without enough money. Now, we enjoy an enormously better lifestyle because of our business. All of this has become tax deductible and we have extra income on top of that.

"It's a great way to raise a family. Frank and I arrived home from a meeting one night to find a sign in our kitchen that the kids had made on their computer. It read, "Thanks for working so hard Mom and Dad!" It was decorated with dollar signs. They understand where we are going with this business."

Exotic Business Strategy

Ryan Vanderpool's entire family is going places with their TTP business — really fun places. One of their business-building strategies is vacationing in exotic locations.

Ryan elaborates, "Like any business owners, if we go on a trip or a vacation, we try to figure out how to make it tax deductible. Through my TTP business, I learned that I could write off my Jamaican vacation if I could justify why I was in Jamaica and that I was working the business.

"I knew I had to have documented evidence that I had talked to other people about The Tax People while in Jamaica. I started approaching people, and it worked out better than I first imagined."

Ryan continues, "The first person I talked to was a man sitting poolside. I introduced myself and I asked him what he did for his living. After he told me, he asked what I did for a living. I told him that I helped people save money on their taxes. His reaction was, 'Oh, really?'"

Ryan repeated this process over-and-over until he had met nearly everyone at the resort. "Everyone I spoke to wanted to know more. I told them that I was on vacation and didn't have time to tell them much right now. I had pen and paper with me — imagine that — and we swapped names and numbers. I promised to call them once I was back in the states."

In addition to a sizable number of qualified prospects, Ryan returned home with written evidence that his travels had a business purpose.

Climbing The Hills Of Success With Dune Buggies?

Ray and Debbie Myers didn't realize all the perks that come with operating a TTP business when they became customers in 1997. Ray talks about his family: "We race sand dune buggies and four-wheel ATV's. Debbie and I both have dune buggies and our two boys each have a four-wheeler. I've always believed these expenses could be tax deductible. Once a customer, I called The Tax People and asked how I could make this happen."

In addition to writing off their dune buggies, ATV's and the fifth-wheel trailer, the Myers also wanted to deduct the expenses associated with their sport. The Myers spoke to Tom Steelman, a tax expert on TTP's Tax Dream Team. Ray reasons, "Big companies write-off yachts. With the fifth-wheel trailer, we write-off a yacht on wheels."

Tax People customers learn how to legally take personal expenses and convert them into tax deductible business expenses. The result can be an incredible amount of money that is freed to spend on other things beside taxes.

The Myers used this strategy. They had a new fifth-wheel trailer custom built to haul their sand buggies and legally lowered their taxes because they deducted it as a business expense according to the IRS Tax Code and Regulations.

Ray paints a picture for us: "It's bright red with The Tax People emblems and advertising slogans across the side. Wherever we go to ride the dune buggies and ATV's, people ask us about the message on our trailer."

The Myers use their ATV's to prospect in their targeted market of sand buggy enthusiasts. Ray feels confident that, "If you have horses, motorcycles or race cars, The Tax People can show you the legal method to make what you love doing tax deductible. Every time I spend money on dune riding, I'm saving money on my taxes. You can do the same."

Ray shares his experiences: "We pull the trailer into sports meets, trailer parks and truck stops. I guarantee people come up and ask, 'What's this all about? What's this trailer? What is this tax deal?' We designed it for that purpose and it works very, very well."

Daughter's Dental Work Becomes Tax Deductible

Like the Myers, Annette Laffey was also surprised what she could legally deduct from her taxes. She explains, "I had just started my own hypnotherapy business. I was talking on the phone with a close friend from Chicago. She told me that $1,600 worth of braces for my daughter Netasha could be tax deductible. I thought she was nuts, but I had to find out for myself."

Annette discovered her friend was correct and tells us, "The Tax People showed me how to legally turn personal expenses into business expenses. It wasn't about taking money out of my pocket; it was about putting it back in. I joined The Tax People and used their services. Then my husband Rick, who is a locksmith, received a $400 per month net take-home pay raise. I'm putting that money in mutual funds for my three children's college educations."

Annette was so excited that she began to tell her friends and family. They were very interested. Annette was thrilled at the response she was receiving: "They were able to understand and use The Tax People strategies to increase their take-home pay. When I saw that, I put my hypnotherapy business on hold to work The Tax People full-time."

Let Go Of Your Limits And They Will Let Go Of You

Danna Spratling's life also changed as a result of her Tax People business. She was a realtor when she first became a TTP customer during April 1999.

She remarks, "I had just sold $1,000,000 in real estate in one month. Over the past two years, I had sold 150 homes. When I saw The Tax People, I realized that if I had helped 150 people have access to this service, instead of just one-time paychecks, I could have been financially set."

Danna's real estate expertise was with investment properties and foreclosures. It opened her eyes as she explains, "I met families losing their homes. Or I would take clients to loan officers and it was amazing their debt loads: credit cards, car payments and mortgages. In most homes, if one or the other spouse had lost his or her job, the families would have been in foreclosure unless they could sell fast."

Each day, Danna worked with the same challenge. "People want the biggest house and the lowest payment. Families are so strapped by debt, and I wasn't helping their situations. That was part of the reason I wanted out of real estate."

According to a survey published in *Newsweek* on December 8, 1999, on average, 63% of women come to a point of reflection in their lives and choose to place priority on helping others. Danna found herself among that majority.

Danna recalls that it was TTP's Women Masterminds that first caught her eye. "It is amazing how many women The Tax People has helped. The mastermind group shows women who have been out of the workforce or lack support how to get back on their feet. If women are looking at this and have no experience but have desire in their hearts, then they can succeed."

Danna knows first-hand about the desire to succeed. She reveals something she has shared with few people: "I understand how frightened women can feel. Five years ago at 26-years-old, I lost my husband to drugs and alcohol. He had no life insurance. I scrambled to take care of our two young children and pay over $16,000 in debts.

"I didn't want to be on welfare, but I needed to feed my children. I was on food stamps for six months. I hated it and was so embarrassed that I would go grocery shopping at midnight.

"With welfare, people are limited in how much money they can earn before they lose food off their tables or daycare for their children. I started my career in real estate because I didn't want to get caught up in the system. In order to earn a living, I found myself spending a great deal of time away from my children. I just wish I had known about The Tax People sooner. This business is the perfect way off welfare.

"Parents can earn significant money quickly working from home while taking care of their children" — a statement that Danna can make from experience as she and her three children Kailan,13, Kelsea, 10, and Max,1, enjoy the financial success of their home-based business.

While some people wish they could work from home, other people wish they had a home to work from.

Tali Mauai and his wife Josey were fighting the high cost of living in their home state of Hawaii. Even though he had a job, it seemed a losing battle as he confesses, "We actually lived on the beach. No house. No car. No phone. It was embarrassing to pretend we just arrived at the beach when we ran into our friends.

"Josey and I prayed on the beach many nights. The Tax People was the answer to our prayers. When we found this business, we went to work. Every hour that we have spent in our TTP business has turned out to be a step towards our American Dream."

Tali was looking for a miracle when he and Josey started their TTP business. A previous business experience had left him unsure and desperate. "The other network marketing company that I was involved with paid me ¼ of 1 percent of my customers' phone calls. My income after seriously building that business for 4-years was $11 per month."

Comparing his telecommunications business to his current, "My TTP business is much easier. I asked a few people if they wanted pay raises and was surprised how quickly they enrolled. In the beginning, all I knew was that people got pay raises and the company did the taxes. Then, four days later I got my first check for $100. More $100 checks followed. That blew me away. In my other company, I worked years for $11. In The Tax People, I worked minutes for $100."

Tali details his first experiences: "I was still new in the business when I made an appointment to show the company video to my friend Fern. When I arrived at her house, I put the video in the VCR and pushed play. You know what happened? The machine ate the video. My heart nearly stopped.

"Fern must have seen how nervous I felt as I fumbled around not knowing what to do. She said, 'Tali, if it will help me on my taxes, go ahead and sign me up.'

"As she was writing a check, her son's friend, John, walked into the house asking, 'Fern, do you know anyone who does taxes?'"

To his amazement Tali explains, "I couldn't believe it! I helped Fern enroll John as a customer of The Tax People. TTP's experts helped John receive an immediate net take-home pay raise of $450 a month."

Tali worked at a local hospital where he met Wendy Cox, a single mother of two children. She had just become a representative of a network marketing telecommunication company. Tali wanted to talk to her about The Tax People. She wanted to talk about the telecommunications company.

Tali told her, "If you get paid in 60 days, I will listen to you about your company. If you don't get paid in 60 days, then you have to listen to me about The Tax People." She agreed.

Sixty days later, Wendy was listening to Tali and received an immediate net take-home pay raise of $380 a month.

Amazed and wanting to help others, Wendy had the idea to host a TTP meeting at her home for people who were interested in immediate pay raises. Tali lead the meeting for six of Wendy's friends. Half way through, Tali was interrupted when the guests asked for applications. Everyone enrolled.

Wendy had experienced immediate success. She had earned $600 in bonuses that night from retail sales of the *Tax Relief System*.

Her home-based business income began to grow. It allowed Wendy to move from her tiny, old apartment to a spacious, new townhome.

Wendy's business continued to grow until her townhome wasn't large enough to handle the folks coming to hear about The Tax People. Tali smiles as he recalls, "To have room for everyone, we had to move our meetings to the local country club. We told everyone that they could bring guests. We reserved a room for 30 people and 173 showed. It was standing room only. We all wore our flower leis and made it the official grand opening of The Tax People in Hawaii."

That week, at the hospital where Tali worked, he was assisting an employee named Louana. Tali became very concerned. "She was so thin, maybe a little over 100 pounds. I asked her why she was so skinny. Louana told me that she had 3 jobs and 2 babies. Her husband worked on another island. They were struggling to make ends meet."

Tali explained The Tax People's services to Louana. She wanted to both purchase the *Tax Relief System* and help others learn about the many benefits.

Tali agreed to help. He explains Louana's first day in the business: "The Tax People has a newspaper that Independent Marketing Associates can hand out. I gave her a stack telling her to write her name and phone number on each paper. I drove Louana to a local clinic where she dropped the papers on the news rack inside the lobby door."

Shortly after Tali and Louana left the newspapers, a woman walked into the clinic, noticed the papers and grabbed one. She read the newspaper, found Louana's phone number and called.

Tali had just dropped Louana off at her home when she heard the phone ring. Louana ran into the house, over to the phone and picked it up. The voice at the other end said, "Louana, I worked for the IRS."

Surrounded by tropical warmth, a chill of fear ran through Louana's body. The voice continued, "I'm reading this newspaper. Tell me more about your company."

Louana panicked, "I don't know anything about any company."

The former IRS employee questioned, "Why is your name on the paper?"

Scanning her mind for a reason, Louana blurted, "Some guy by the name of Tali told me to write my name and number on it."

The former agent directed, "I want you to call that man named Tali and give him my address. I want to see him at my house this Sunday at noon."

Shaken and ready to run, Louana called Tali. Worried from the last conversation and angry that she had listened to Tali, she fired-off, "Tali, I feel *sorry* for *you*. The IRS is looking for you. Somebody from the IRS read the newspaper and she want *you* at *her* house this Sunday."

As he listened to Louana, Tali grabbed a pen and paper and wrote down the address for the Sunday afternoon meeting. Knowing that TTP's Tax Dream Team was comprised of former IRS employees, Tali relaxed.

Sunday came. With courage in his heart, Tali and his wife drove through pouring rain to arrive at the IRS mystery house. Tali outlines what his game plan was: "I didn't call ahead to see what they wanted. I just went to meet the IRS woman with my TTP video in hand."

When he walked in, three stone-faced people sat in the living room. Tali recalls, "I was not received well."

Assuming they wanted more information about the company, Tali offered, "Let's look at the video."

Tali describes what happened next, "The IRS lady's husband and the other man in the room fell asleep." They snored so loudly that I couldn't hear the video."

The former IRS woman kept watching. When the video was complete she began asking questions: "Is this legal? Is this a pyramid? Is this a scam?"

Tali answered from his heart telling stories of how families he knew were being helped by The Tax People.

The former IRS employee, her husband and their friend became customers that day. Tali remarks, "From then on, our organization grew like wild-fire. In one year, Josey and I had 769 people in our group."

Their income is growing dramatically surpassing $6,000 a month. Tali gives thanks, "Coming from being homeless on the beach, Josey and I are truly grateful for this kind of money.

"We are buying a 3,200 square foot, 5-bedroom home with three full baths. It is much, much bigger than where we live now. Before The Tax People, there was no way we would look at that kind of home."

About other benefits Tali says, "We bought a 2000 Chevy Venture mini-van with all the toys. The Tax People makes the payments. It feels so good. It's the fanciest car we have ever ridden. People know this business is real because Josey and I are driving that van."

Earning more money does enhance people's lives. Yet, all that "money talk" often gives way to the real benefits of TTP businesses.

Tali's voice slows as he tells more: "For 15 years, my wife and I have been trying to have our first child. I believe the universe knows that if a child is given, parents must have the means to provide care.

"When we did not have money or a home, there was no baby. Suddenly TTP comes to our lives. Now, we make money and have a home. Then, we discovered that Josey and I have a baby on the way. How *fabulous* that is!"

Tali shares his deeper sentiments: "I think that TTP is heaven sent. I believe that CEO Michael Cooper and Vice President Todd Strand are on a mission to help the human race.

"There has never been a company like this. From the president to the corporate office support staff, Independent Marketing Associates receive 100% support.

"The Tax People provides families with immediate and long-term money. Since I became a TTP customer, I have entered homes of the poor and the middle-class. I have sat across tables from millionaires. People in all types of financial situations have become customers and, within a week, called me to say thank you."

Tali sums up, "Sometimes I take people to the beach and show them the sand where Josey and I used to sleep. I tell them that we came from this place. We are so grateful to TTP and the people who gave us a better life.

"Before living in Hawaii, I came from the island of Samoa by Tahiti. I knew nothing about network marketing, but I did about poverty. My parents died in poverty. I'm 46-years-old. I know that I will have money and be able to provide for my family for the rest of my life and beyond. I am thankful for that opportunity."

Nasser Moussa is the Assistant Director of Operations for The Tax People. He understands the importance of opportunity and talks about American freedoms often taken for granted.

He left his homeland in Israel for college in the United States. After graduating with an accounting degree, he chose to stay. He's candid about his decision: "In Israel there are more prejudices than most people can imagine. For the most part, the citizens are either Jewish or Arab. To be an Arab in Israel is very difficult."

Nasser illustrates by comparison, "America is a free country; Israel is not. In America, people can say whatever they want. That can't be done in Israel. People must be very careful what they say and how they say it."

"Since I have lived in America, I have not had a problem with prejudice. As a foreigner, I have never had anyone make me feel like I didn't belong. In Israel, the minute I walked out of my home I could feel it, even though I was born there."

Nasser compares the opportunities in America to those in Israel. "If I wanted a job like the one I have here, the company would have to be owned by an Arab. There were not many opportunities for Arabic people.

"I love America. There are many opportunities for people regardless of age, gender, education, skin color or any other challenges. People can succeed in America."

Our country is known as the land of opportunity and prosperity. The first place most people look for indications of a strong economy is the stock market. With the Dow roaring from under 4000 in 1994 to closing over 11,000 during 1999, our bullish economy has bred success after success.

But, what kind is it?

The New Webster's Dictionary defines success as " a person who or a thing that attains a desired end." Newsstands flourish with magazines guaranteeing success by being your own boss. Awards are handed out to those who achieve entrepreneurship's top ranks.

But, are all those award winners really winning in the real game of life?

David & Crystal Hart are owners of the Waxman, an auto-detailing business and 1992 winners of the Southern California Entrepreneur of the Year Award.

For 14 years, David Hart was content operating his stressful and physically demanding auto-detailing business. One sudden event forever changed his point of view. David received a phone call that his 52-year-old father had died of a heart attack at work.

On top of the family's shock and pain, they discovered that David's father had not made provisions for his retirement or death. To survive, David's mother was forced into the workplace.

It had become painfully obvious to David that he was quickly heading down the same path as his father. David used his father's death as the driving force behind his own desire to create financial security rather than his own paycheck-to-paycheck charade.

The auto-detailing business was consuming his family. "Crystal and I both worked full-time in our Waxman business. Our kids were in daycare. Here we were entrepreneurs — the people who have control over their lives — with no control and someone else raising our children."

Money was so tight that Crystal worked in their business with no pay. "Our marriage was suffering

The Tax People CEO Michael Cooper with his son, Clint, deep sea fishing off the Big Island of Hawaii, September 1999.

CEO Michael Cooper's wife Mary with son Colby on Waikiki Beach, September 1999.

"He ain't heavy, he's my brother!" Clint Cooper holding
Colby Cooper outside of The Tax People business meeting.

Taylor McLaughlin holds TTP *Tax Relief System*
that put three shopping carts of toys under his
family's Christmas tree (story page 34).

The Pay Raise Picnic hosted by Irany and Pablo Dibello (pg. 16).

The Michael and Mary Cooper family from (l to r)
Front row: daughter Christa Moussa, son Colby Cooper, Mary
Cooper, son Robert Cooper, Robert's fiancée Rhonda Browning.
ack row: son-in-law Nasser Moussa, Michael Cooper, son Clint Cooper.

The Hutchinsons are among many families who are now earning a sizable income by both parents working from their home while raising their children. (l to r) Rachel, Greyson, Steve, Gwyneth, Janet, Rebekah (pg. 98).

Crystal, Wayne III, Melinda, Wayne Jones. Executive Assistant & IMA Melinda Jones joined the home office team January 2000.

Annette Laffey and her family used the *Tax Relief System* to legally deduct $1,600 for Netasha's braces. Plus, Rick received an instant $400 increase in his take-home pay. Front row (l to r) Netasha, Amanda-Rae, (pup) Buddy, Brian. Back row Annette, Rick (pg. 116).

Single parent Kathleen Baska, full-time mom, earns her living via her home-based business. (l to r) Michael, Marya, Kathleen and Karl (pg. 177).

Marco Santos, Jr.'s family is thankful he advised them to use The Tax People when they were audited. Within two days, the audit was resolved over the phone without the Santos even talking to the IRS. (l to r) Marco, Sr.; Marisela; Claudia; Blanca; Marco, Jr. (pg. 195).

Ying Yang and his family escaped his homeland during wartime. His TTP business supports his family of 13.

BOARD OF DIRECTORS

Michael Cooper, CEO and Founder, Renaissance and The Tax People is one of the most experienced corporate network marketing executives in America; a member of Mensa and published author; computer genius who was first in industry to develop software to pay bonuses daily, weekly and monthly.

Mr. James H. Carter, Chairman of the Board of Directors, co-founded American Investors Life Insurance, served as its first President from 1965 until 1974. He served as Vice President for TVC Marketing which offered Pre-Paid Legal Services through a large organization of independent marketing representatives (pg. 50).

Richard Dahms, J.D. was a 1953 graduate of Central Missouri State University. Judge Dahms received his Juris Doctorate Degree from the University of Missouri in 1956. He has served as Missouri Assistant Attorney General, Probate Court Judge, Buchanan County Missouri Assistant Prosecuting Attorney, Public Defender Fifth Judicial Circuit Missouri (pg. 49).

BOARD OF DIRECTORS

Attorney Mary Joe Smith was a former Missouri Assistant Attorney General for six years and currently operates her own successful legal practice (pg. 23, 206).

Dr. Michael Muscatella is a practicing podiatrician who graduated in 1987 Cum Laude from W.M. Sholl College of Podiatric Medicine, is a diplomat of the American Board of Podiatric Surgery and fellow of the American College of Foot Surgeons. He has served on the faculty of the University of Illinois College of Medicine. Dr. Muscatella has received the Williams & Wilkins Award for Academic and Clinical Excellence in Surgery.

Don W. John received his Bachelor of Science in Business Administration at Southwestern University, Weathorford, Oklahoma. He is engaged in various business ventures including real estate, insurance and other investments. He is active in church, civic and charitable organizations.

Jesse Cota, National Director of Taxes for TTP, is a 33-year IRS veteran and retired District Director of the IRS Southern California District. Respect for people is a high priority to Jesse. While with the IRS, Jesse directed his employees to both "treat people like people" and respect taxpayers' rights. In his present position, he is a member of a team that provides tax answers to TTP's customers. Jesse, a CPA, works closely with TTP's affiliate tax professionals in sharing its home-based business tax strategies with TTP's customers (pg. 1, 66, 78, 193, 203, 233).

Thomas W. Steelman, one of TTP's Tax Dream Team leaders, graduated from Southern Missouri State with both BS and Masters degrees in business/accounting tax. He passed his CPA exam in 1978 as a revenue agent and was promoted through the highest ranks of the IRS until he chose to retire after 28 years. As an enrolled agent, Steelman can represent and defend taxpayers in IRS situations without the individuals being present. TTP members are greatly relieved to find that, when it comes to dealing with tax authorities like the IRS, Steelman and his colleagues can do all the talking and negotiating (pg. 191, 195).

Jeff Schnepper is the author of *How to Pay Zero Taxes* (17th edition, McGraw-Hill). He is Microsoft's tax expert for their Web site. He co-authored *Microsoft Money* and *Turbo Tax Deluxe*. Mr. Schnepper is one of America's most highly respected tax experts. He holds two law degrees and an MBA in finance. He is one of The Tax People's tax strategists and advisors verifying that the *Tax Relief System* provides people with accurate and valid tax advice (foreword).

(l to r) Anthony, Annette, Paul, Tom and Salvatore Silvio. Two years into their TTP business, the Silvios have afforded a new home double the size of their previous home. Their TTP business is earning enough that both Tom and Annette work from home (pg. 84).

Lyndsey, Amber, Bob and Jimmy Schaffer used TTP's *Tax Relief System* to receive an immediate pay raise of $1,000 per month and still received an additional $12,700 refund. They also replaced their $240,000 income with earnings from their TTP home-based business (pg. 108).

When Greg Alexander's heart stopped and he was hospitalized for weeks, his family continued to receive the $2,400 monthly check from his TTP business even though he was unable to work (pg. 12, 166).

Tom Kehne's part-time TTP business earns him over $50,000 a year in addition to his income as a professional pilot. The first year that Tom used the *Tax Relief System* he saved $11,000 in taxes (pg. 100).

(l to r) Daughter Karlista, Jeannie, Bill and son Chad. Bill and Jeannie Greenfield used the *Tax Relief System* & personal advice from the Tax Dream Team to save $8,441 on their 1998 taxes. The Greenfields employ their teens for $4,250 each. It is money they would have spent anyway, but now it's tax free to the kids and 100% deductible for the parents. The kids work the family's TTP business along with their parents (pg. 70, 179).

Son Brandon, daughter Brandi, Renee and Benny Brown. Benny and Renee saved $14,000 by using the *Tax Relief System*. They told a friend who used the services of The Tax People to receive a $43,000 refund on his previously filed taxes that The Tax People amended (pg. 58).

Michael Cooper relaxing by pouring a concrete drive
at his 100-acre family ranch.

Michael Cooper's favorite toy. Years ago, Michael's goal was to have a
John Deere riding lawn mower. Today, he has the whole tractor!

Mary and Michael Cooper. Graduation May 1999, Mary received her Masters Degree in social work. After Mary's many hours of academic dedication, the Coopers have a life together again.

Michael and Mary Cooper on their way to Sturgis, South Dakota Motorcycle Rally, August 1999.

Irany and Pablo Dibello build their business by having fun! They host the parties that everyone wants to attend: Pay Raise Picnics (pg. 180).

Art and Jackie Hebner happily celebrate their 50th wedding anniversary. Another happy note is the result of a recent IRS audit where, previously, Art had mistakenly burned his receipts. The Tax People worked on Art's behalf citing tax code and law. The IRS agreed to let Art's tax return stand as originally prepared (pg. 189, 192).

Life is more than just work! The Tax People 4th of July party with "Wild West" entertainment. Mr. James Carter is caught in the middle. Mary Cooper (right), Sheryl Tasker (far right) and two other "Wild Women of the Frontier" on the left.

Celebrating tax savings Hawaiian style!
(l to r) Back row: Richard Colburn, Deborah Robarts (pg. 73), Matt Briseno (pg. 216), Annabelle Briseno, Mary Cooper, Michael Cooper. Front row: Clint Cooper and Colby Cooper.

Prior to becoming TTP customers, Norma and Troy Cruse mortgaged their home to pay a $10,000 debt the IRS claimed the couple owed. Then, using the services of The Tax People, the Cruses discovered the IRS actually owed them $11,000! (pg. 190).

The Harts (l to r) daughter Katie, Crystal, son Justin holding family dog, son Joshua and David. The Harts used their TTP business to buy back their time. David and Crystal are now Dad and Mom again (pg. 128).

Steve Kassel (l) and Darryl Roberts (r). Nationally renowned tax expert Steve Kassel resolves problems for taxpayers who owe the IRS. He has been the tax expert on *Good Morning America, New York Times* and *CNN Financial Network* (pg. 229). Darryl Roberts and his wife Maria used TTP's services to quickly resolve a sizable tax problem and are very successful IMA's (pg. 198).

Lora Lee Manikam is Director of Affiliated Tax Professionals. Previously, she was an H&R Block executive. She hosts TTP's Tax Professionals Call where she explains how tax firms are increasing their incomes by thousands – some over $100,000 annually by completing TTP customers' returns (pg. 75, 219).

(l to r) Johnny MacNaught, Lora Lee Manikam and Mr. James Carter. Johnny MacNaught is Vice President of Field Operations. He coordinates TTP's tax affiliate program (pg. 38).

Tax professional Frankie Ruth was one of the first TTP tax experts. Within her first year, her practice doubled in volume with healthy profit margins (pg. 224).

Jim and Judy Fletcher. Judy is an income tax professional who has prepared thousands of returns over her 20-year career (pg. 206).

Scott Turner is a 20-year CPA veteran and lead tax expert for a legal firm with 5.2 million clients (pg. 211).

Major General James Rueger was nominated to the post of 2-Star Army General by President Bush and Commanding General of Missouri's 9,000 member Army and Air National Guards by the governor. He believes highly in TTP services. As a customer, during his first six months, he saved $4,500 in taxes because of legal deductions of which he was unaware (pg. 44).

Bill Helming, highly-respected national economist and recognized by the Cato Institute, Washington D.C., as one of America's top fundamental tax reform experts. In 1985 he wrote the NCT tax reform plan that the Cato Institute selected as the number one alternative to the current tax system. He has been working with Bill Archer, Chairman of the House Ways and Means Committee, the Congressional Subcommittee on Tax Reform and George W. Bush. He is a TTP customer (pg. 2, 63).

(l to r) Chamla Brown and mother Pat Brown. Chamla i Director of Executive Services for TTP and works side-by-side with CEO Michael Cooper (PG. 175). Pat Brown is TTP's receptionist and has been with the company since April 1998.

(l to r) Vice President Johnny MacNaught (pg. 38), Vice President Todd Strand (pg. 77), and Director of Field Operations G.J. Reynolds (pg. 204).

Vice President Sarah Guetschow enrolled her parents who used TTP's services to legally save $18,000 in capital gains taxes on a property sale (pg. 1, 74).

l to r) Diamond Coordinator Daniel Fienhage with Director of Operations Christa Moussa who has been with The Tax People since its origin (pg. 40).

(l to r) Creative Director Larry Stocker and Susie Stacy. Larry feels within three years, TTP will be the household name in the tax industry just as H&R Block was in the last decade (pg. 41).

Art Director Wayne Keeling believes at the current rate, TTP will grow larger than H&R Block or any other tax preparation company (pg. 43).

CEO Michael Cooper wrapping presents for The Tax People
staff holiday party. He gave away over $300,000
in holiday bonuses for Christmas 1999.

Mary and Michael Cooper with Mary's parents, Fred and
Rosemary Spalding, enjoying a ride through New York City.

Curtis and Martha Burgess have been a husband and wife team for 34 years. They were the 31st members to join The Tax People hosting the first TTP business meeting. They've been able to retire from several time, stress and investment intensive businesses that they previously owned.  Their significant TTP earnings has replace their other incomes (pg. 33).

Mary and Michael Cooper enjoying a short break in New York City.

Troy and Tricia Helming received $21,000 in refunds on past taxes that Troy's CPA unknowingly had Troy overpay (pg. 63).

Kim and Kent McLaughlin's TTP enterprise has developed into a $1,000,000 annual home-based business (pg. 60, 84).

The Tax People were the answer to Denise and Tom Nash's prayers. With major IRS problems, the Nashes feel TTP is the most powerful option available to people who want to clean up their pasts and get back into the taxpaying system (pg. 197).

(l to r) Pam, Tara, Frank and J.C. Leonard. Prior to their TTP business, Pam and Frank were lucky to earn $3,000 a month working 16 hours a day, 7 days a week. Today, they make more money than working four jobs (pg. 111, 168).

The Cooks received immediate $800 net take-home pay raises each month. After six months of building their TTP business, they purchased a new home and two new vehicles (pg. 67, 199).

Ryan Vanderpool and family replaced his annual six-figure income
with the earnings from their TTP home-based business.
Now they vacation at exotic locations (pg. 86, 113, 201).

Buck and Nancy Murphy with their family. The Murphys have discovered
that "retirement" can be very lucrative. The Murphys are making more
with their TTP business than from their previous positions (pg. 172).

Hank Oliveira is succeeding in his TTP business despite little formal education. His experiences with The Tax People tell him that he has found a true friend in Michael Cooper (pg. 182).

Pittsburgh Steelers 1975 and 1976 Super Bowl champion player and successful businessman Charles Davis says his respect for Michael Cooper was the reason he took a serious look at TTP (pg. 55, 196).

TTP member and World Champion Earl Christy was a member of the New York Jets and played with Joe Namath when they won the 1969 Super Bowl III. Earl has hosted *EC Sports Network* for 30 years. Active in network marketing, Earl has found that The Tax People has been better by comparison than that of any other companies (pg. 56).

TTP member Earl Christy in action 1969. Earl caught the opening kick-off in Super Bowl III and returned it for 26 yards.

Chicago Bears football player Dave Hale and wife Nori. After four years on the front lines of the Chicago Bears, David's football pension is less than $500 a month. After two years in his TTP business, his residual income is 4-figures a month (pg. 162).

David Hale #75, Chicago Bears Football team 1969 to 1974. This picture shows him pursuing O.J. Simpson of the Buffalo Bills.

Rhonda Browning, Chamla Brown and Sheryl Tasker enjoy The Tax People's Leadership Conference, February 1998.

Dave and Susie Robins used TTP's *Tax Relief System* to legally save $10,000 on their taxes. Their TTP home-based business generates a significant income (pg. 78).

Annette Laffey and Michael Accurso relaxing after a busy day at a TTP convention. Michael is a partner in the MSA group with Kent McLaughlin and Tom Silvio (pg. 84).

By reviewing the *Tax Relief System,* Kathy Coover discovered her CPA had let her overpay her taxes by $30,000 for the last five years. She figured other people had the same problem. By her third month in her TTP business she was earning a high-four figure per month income. Kathy became the first and fastest female Diamond in the Tax People (pg. 77, 90, 204).

CEO Michael Cooper lunching with Independent Marketing Associates in San Diego.

Kay Marovich feels TTP is one of America's most marketable services because everyone wants to legally pay fewer taxes.

Kevin and Cathy Hart used the *Tax Relief System* to discover they had over-paid their taxes $25,000 for the last five years. They also used the *Tax Relief System* to save a friend and her family from bankruptcy (pg. 71).

The Tax People has showed Debbie and Ray Myers how to use their dune buggies and all-terrain vehicles in their TTP business and legally deduct the expenses associated with their sport. The Myers are saving an incredible amount of money in taxes each time they go racing (pg. 114).

Using the *Tax Relief System,* Bill & Amanda Fox saved almost $23,000 in taxes. Bill requested that his step-father review the system resulting in his step-father receiving a $24,000 refund (pg. 75, 203).

because of the unbearable stress. David fired me numerous times, but we couldn't afford to hire my replacement. The Waxman business was slowly killing us both mentally and physically."

Dave interjects, "I was so caught up in what I was doing for my family that I lost touch with them. At work and at home, all the stress I had inside of me came out. The one person I wanted to have patience with, Crystal, I'd have no patience left for."

When the Harts were told about the life-changing possibilities of a TTP business, they had no spare time available. They also realized that they had no choice but to try.

David believed by working their TTP business he could create enough additional income to reduce his 70-hour work week. "Working our Tax People business about 12 hours a week over the course of 11 months has bought back all of Crystal's time and a majority of mine. I've been able to hire a manager to run our Waxman business. Now that my stress level has been lowered, I have the time to let Crystal and the kids know how much I care about them."

Last summer, while the Harts' children were on school break, they vacationed as a family for the entire summer. Crystal shares the significance of this change: "When the Waxman business was our only income, Dave and I vacationed separately. I would take the kids and go somewhere. He would stay and run our auto detailing business. Then, he would vacation and I would run the business. We would never go anywhere together because we couldn't afford to leave our business."

She talks about life since they chose to start their TTP business: "Now we do nearly everything together. This business has allowed David to attend ball games, do homework with kids at night and be there for them when they leave and come home from school."

Crystal observes, "David has changed since we started our TTP business. He's relaxed. We smile and laugh together all the time. All I ever wanted in life was peace. It finally came when we built this business. It gave David the opportunity to once again become the man I had fallen in love with and married."

Success Is More Than Making A Buck; It's Making A Difference

A majority of America wants what Crystal and Dave now have. In a *Newsweek* magazine survey, 89% of the respondents cited the chance to "have a good family life" as their number one priority.

Former Chicago Bears football player Dave Hale describes himself as "intensely pro-family." He and his wife Nori started their Tax People business February 1998 to help their family and others.

For years Nori had the family's tax returns completed by a local CPA. Dave's interest in taxes was less than zero so when tax time arrived, Dave would trudge along to their accountant's office where he tried to stay awake.

Prior to joining, when Dave was asked to attend a business meeting about taxes, he thought, "I think I have to wash my hair that night."

After a little persuasion, Dave agreed to attend. Having been his own boss for years, David found the idea of making money from home to be an everyday occurrence. He describes what flipped the switch in his mind, "During Michael Cooper's presentation, I realized that I had a tax hole at the bottom of my financial bucket. Money was pouring out. When I saw I could legally stop my losses, The Tax People made sense to me — certainly enough sense to get started."

Dave also discovered that he could make income by helping others save money on their taxes. David has found building his TTP business a much easier way to make a living compared to being knocked down in the NFL. After four years on the front lines of the Chicago Bears, David's football pension is less than $500 per month.

"When I first started my TTP business, my goal was to make $1,000 a month part-time. That came pretty quickly. Now, after less than two years with The Tax People, my residual income is 4-figures a month!"

CASHING IN,
SLOWING DOWN,
LIVING BETTER

"To make a living is no longer enough.
Work also has to make a life."
— **Peter Drucker**

On workaholic highs, many Baby-Boomers are experiencing sobering messages as they enter stages of life where they meet evidence of mortality. Their own illnesses and brushes with death, in addition to those of loved ones, are quickly forcing an epidemic of personal priority reshuffling.

Following behind are the Generation-Xers, many of whom were neglected as children while their Boomer parents were spending today's hours chasing tomorrow's power, promotions and prestige. Gen-Xers have watched the enormous prices their parents have paid endlessly postponing personal lives.

It was a brush with death that forced Baby Boomer Greg Alexander to reevaluate the price he was paying.

November 19, 1999 was unseasonably warm when Greg, a TTP customer, stopped by his local grocery store for supper. Tired from running all day, he navigated his shopping cart through the crowded isles to the checkout counter. He stood waiting to pay for his selections as a hot flash of pain overcame his body and his legs gave out. Uncontrollable fear was the last thing Greg remembered before his body hit the floor with the force of a sledgehammer.

Immediately, one of the grocery store personnel called an ambulance while another checked to find Greg wasn't breathing. Thinking quickly, someone made an announcement over the store speakers: "We have a man down who needs CPR. If there is anyone who can help please come to the front quick!"

As time fleeted the crowd circling Greg was disrupted by a woman announcing, "I'm a doctor; move aside."

Her petite body manually forced Greg's heart to disburse the oxygen she blew into his lungs. When the emergency medics arrived, Greg's heart was working only because the woman kept it pumping. The medics used a defibrillator to shock him back to life. Over the course of the coming weeks Greg had a quadruple bypass and a pacemaker implant.

During their near loss, Greg's family continued to receive the $2,400 monthly check from his TTP business.

Greg shares with gratitude, "Thank God for my TTP business. If it weren't for the residual income from this business, my family would have been financially destroyed. My health had been going downhill for some time. February 1998 I was diagnosed with thyroid, kidney and water retention problems. November 1998 I was diagnosed with a heart problem. A year later, my heart stopped completely.

"There have been many times over the past two years that if I didn't have the residual income each month from my TTP business, it would have been very tough for my family. Even with my past health challenges, working part-time from home, I'm able to earn $2,400 a month. That money comes forever, whether I am able to work or not. Tax-wise, the last two years, TTP has saved my family over $12,000."

Greg figures, "At this point, I'm 47-years-old and realize that I can't get life insurance. I have some, but now I am super-uninsurable. After this episode, I realize how quickly life can change or end. I want to make sure my family is taken care of when my time comes. Realizing this, all the time I was in the hospital, I kept talking about The Tax People to the nurses, doctors and preachers. I have 35 prospects from my hospital stays."

Returning home December 1st, Greg started making phone calls to people who had previously voiced an interest in The Tax People. He couldn't get out of his chair, but he could pick up the phone. The first day home, Greg enrolled a new Independent Marketing Associate.

Greg says with reassurance, "All my family and friends have a new rededication to building the TTP business. I have a new lease on life now that I've been gone and come back. My family has been brought closer together than ever before. We all realize the importance of each other and providing the family with a sizable on-going income. My wife has taken the business more seriously, and we are working it together."

The Best Way To Quickly Reach Your Destination Is To Take People With You

Husband and wife, Frank and Pam Leonard, joined TTP in September 1998. Frank was a territory manager for the National Federation of Independent Businesses (NFIB), a well-respected federal lobbying organization for small business owners. His income from NFIB fluctuated because he worked on commission. Pam had recently retired from 15 years in the banking industry to become a stay-home-mom for their kids, J.C. who was 8-years-old and Tara who was 13.

Frank talks about why they joined TTP: "We were existing on my up-and-down income. The tax strategies we implemented as a result of starting our TTP business brought my family an immediate take-home pay raise of about $400 a month. That was a real blessing for our family!"

During their second month in their TTP business, Frank and Pam spoke with a young couple from Orange

County, California. Shortly into their conversation, the woman started crying. Perplexed, Pam wrapped an arm around her and asked, "What's wrong?"

Tears fell as the young lady questioned, "Pam, are you telling me for $100 a month, we get an immediate pay raise of $280 a month? We'd have $180 left to spend? I've been praying for a way to pay the utilities that are being shut-off!"

Frank remembers, "It was then that Pam and I realized people really need and want what TTP offers. It's our mission to tell people about TTP. We decided if we never earned one penny, we'd do it anyway. There are families, like ours, who desperately need more money."

Understanding the toll that over-paying taxes can have on a family, Frank explains, "My father lost his business because of IRS issues. I watched him work 18 hours a day, 7 days a week trying to save our family. My father was a burly 250 pounds. By the time he was 72-years-old, fighting the IRS and cancer had left him at 95 pounds."

Frank sadly recalls, "The only place he could find work was at a public storage facility. He and my mother managed it and lived on-site. The cancer forced my father into a bedridden state, but my mother was able to complete all of their responsibilities and manage the facility."

"With no respect for human life, the corporation said that if my cancer-ridden, near-death father didn't get out of bed, they were going to fire him and my mother. This would have left them homeless without an income. In order to keep the roof over their heads and their paycheck, my 95-pound father was painfully forced out of his deathbed to walk the grounds daily.

"By Christmas time, he knew it was only a matter of days before his imminent death. His life insurance policy expired at year-end. He knew that if he lived a week into the new year, they'd lose the life insurance. My father took his own life so that he could leave something for my mother. The IRS had taken everything else that they owned."

Frank chokes, "The public storage fired my mother because she had no spouse. The company wouldn't allow her to manage the property alone. With no income, my mother moved in with my sister and is now bagging groceries at 60-years-old.

"All my life, I wanted more for my parents. I've barely been able to provide for my own family. Personally, I've felt the humiliation of being a penniless father, forced into bankruptcy."

Frank has found a way to help his family. "By the end of 2000, the income from my TTP business will allow me to purchase a new car and home for my mother. In my lifestyle prior to my TTP business, I was lucky if I made $3,000 a month working 16 hours a day, 7 days a week. Today I make more money than I ever made at one time working three or four jobs."

"Last month was our 13th month in the business. Working 25-30 hours a week, Pam and I made $9,300. By our 18th month, we should be earning over $15,000 a month. That's how I know I can afford to help my mother."

Frank reasons, "Everyone wants more for their children, but it seems today we work harder than our parents. I feel that our children will work harder than we worked unless they choose a different path. We have an opportunity to show people how to keep more of their hard-earned money and create financial wealth."

"If our TTP business had only allowed Pam and me to increase my paycheck as an employee by $600 a month, even that would have changed our lives. I would have avoided bankruptcy. We could have bought clothes for the kids. If we hadn't had that immediate pay raise when we started during the holidays of 1998, our kids would have gone without Christmas presents. They've gone without before and it hurt."

Before becoming a customer of The Tax People, Frank lived a very stressful life. "We were just trying to keep our heads above water. Every Sunday night I would pray that I would have a paycheck that week. I worked on commission. I started every Monday with $875 in bills and $0 income. With this business every Monday, I'm facing one month of *paid* bills. I'm saving money in the bank, driving a brand new vehicle and providing whatever my family needs."

In the beginning, when the Leonards were told that their TTP business would provide the opportunity to earn $5,000 and more a month, they didn't believe it. Frank recalls, "We couldn't imagine that kind of money from a part-time business. Pam was just asking for an extra $500. We didn't see our first $500 check. The first check we received was for $1,000.

"I make good money now and I will never forget what it was like not to have money. The beautiful part of this business is that we can immediately increase people's take-home pay and give them back their lives. We give them a path to follow out of the darkness. Everyone in America who pays taxes is already in our business. The only difference between them and us is that they are still paying too much. We have our lives back because we are legally paying only our fair share."

Live All You Can

February 1999 found Buck and Nancy Murphy looking for a way to buy back their lives.

The Murphys own a wholesale clothing business that they started when Buck was 56-years-old. Buck comments, "Companies weren't hiring people who were 56 and older. Nancy and I had to invest $250,000 in our clothing company. We bought ourselves jobs but hadn't created freedom or walk-away income. We do make money but it's not what I'd call fun for a 67-year-old man.

"Society has no place for the elderly. Of all the people in modern history who have lived to 65 and older, 70% of them are alive today. In centuries past, people didn't live that long."

Buck is right. Today's sixty-five-year-olds have many more healthy and active years ahead of them than their 1960 counterparts. They are much more likely to choose early retirement. This results in available time that these mature adults are using to start part-time businesses. These early retirees have thick Rolodexes from lifetimes of informal networking and are finding success in The Tax People.

Mr. Murphy's mission is to inform people that life exists after they have retired. "A TTP business can be started with a very small investment of time and money. Nancy and I have experienced financial success in our TTP business because of how Michael Cooper designed the compensation plan. This is an even playing field. There is no discrimination of any kind.

"I am currently earning over $6,000 per month and my income is increasing every month." In addition to their income, the Murphys will also soon qualify for an additional monthly bonus of $5,000. This, in addition to their other TTP revenues, will allow them to replace their income from the clothing business and buy back their time.

Plus, in less than nine months, the Murphys earned a brand new $65,000 Infiniti Q45 automobile on which The Tax People makes the monthly payments.

Buck summarizes, "We're going to buy condos in Hawaii and here in California. We'll travel between condos visiting our grandchildren, living the good life."

According to *The Futurist* magazine, in the quest to stay eternally young, 64 percent of Baby Boomers say they will remain active in another career after retirement. Of this group who won't quit, 82 percent plan to invest part-time efforts while 11 percent desire new full-time careers.

Commenting on retirement, comedian George Burns once quipped, "Retirement at sixty-five is ridiculous. When I was sixty-five, I still had pimples."

Buck smiles as he elaborates, "Nancy and I are involved, accepted, competing and part of a winning team. We look young. We feel young. We surround ourselves with young people. There are millions of people like us that don't want to pack it in yet. Seniors can't live on Social Security, yet society says we are too old. A TTP business changes all that."

Buck and Nancy investigated The Tax People thoroughly before deciding to become customers. Buck notes, "Older people have been hurt and lied to before. They become cynical, doubtful and hard to convince. Before we agreed to become TTP customers, I had to meet Michael Cooper and The Tax People's Board of Directors.

Remembering that meeting, Buck confesses, "I am a southern California beach person and have spent much of my life living in the fast lane. Meeting Mike Cooper was like meeting a farmer, someone you could trust. He's a regular guy, not pretentious or trying to be someone he's not. It was comforting to know that a Heartland man, not a city slicker, is at the helm of this company."

Chamla Brown, Director of Executive Services for TTP, describes her experiences: "I work side-by-side with Michael Cooper who is one of the most generous humans I have known. I have seen people who are in tough financial or emotional shape who he has helped with empathy, compassion and money. Michael opens his door, his heart and his checkbook. People in need walk in feeling hopeless and walk out with dignity."

"I remember a single mother of an autistic child. Her son needed the advantage of special schooling. There was no way she could afford to keep her child in that special school. It was Michael Cooper who made sure that child received the education he needed. That's only one of dozens of illustrations of Michael's generosity and compassion for others."

"Michael has been equally generous when designing the compensation plan that our Independent Marketing Associates are paid upon. IMA's have many streams of income. One is from the multiple bonus pools where over 10% of the gross residual income of the company is placed in the pools. That's a huge percentage of the total national residual income of the company paid to IMA's as bonuses."

"Towards the end of 1979, there was a bonus pool which no one had yet achieved. Instead of keeping it for the company, as many executives would do, Michael chose to pay it out to the IMA's as surprise Christmas bonuses. Michael split the bonus pool equally among the people who were actively building their businesses. Hundreds of people received unexpected checks in the mail right before Christmas!"

Chamla asks, "Have you ever heard of a network marketing company actually going the extra mile for the people in the field and paying out *MORE* than the compensation plan calls for? Or paying out money that the company can otherwise keep? They almost always seem to horde, heist, or hide money from distributors."

Talking about what she believes has lead to Michael's generous nature, "In 1979 at 25-years-old, Michael lost his wife and was left as a single father raising two babies on his own. After remarrying, times became financially tough again, and he moved his family into a horse barn. Yes, you heard correctly. Michael insulated a portion of it and built bedrooms, a kitchen and a bathroom. Even though he now lives in a beautiful home, the barn still stands as a reminder."

Thinking out loud, Chamla says, "He has the compassionate heart that comes from the pains and joys of overcoming hard times.

"Generosity, honesty and promises kept are the keys to Michael's success. His mind is sharp and Michael works hard, sometimes around the clock for days, to assure that the cornerstones are in place for TTP's Independent Marketing Associates and staff to handle the company's enormous growth.

"In the two years that I have been a part of TTP, I have watched the company grow and enhance multi-fold. The Tax People and Michael Cooper are already creating millionaires and will create thousands more people who are financially successful beyond their largest dreams."

Summarizing, Chamla states, "This is the only business that I have experienced where people can walk off the street, sign their applications and achieve what they thought were their wildest dreams. Anybody who is willing to work will be incredibly successful and their families rewarded."

Don't Let "Well Done" On Your Tombstone Mean You Were Cremated

Many years ago, Kathleen A. Baska operated a vending business that allowed her to work from home when her children were young. One of her major accounts decided not to renew its contract and Kathleen's income suffered.

She explains, "Shortly afterwards, I picked my daughter up at school and told her I would have to start working a 9-to-5 job to pay the bills. She started crying, 'Mom, I want you home with me.' My daughter just wanted to know that I was there. I have met many parents who agree that we must start giving our children roots."

Recently, Kathleen and her husband went through a divorce that greatly upset her two teenagers. It tore her family apart. For the two years prior to her divorce, Kathleen worked full-time outside the home. With their father gone, Kathleen felt she needed to give her children the stability of having at least one parent home.

In April 1999, Kathleen decided to start a house cleaning business figuring she could set her own hours and work while the kids were in school. Amazed by the turn of events, she comments, "Three hours after I had quit my full-time job to start my new business, my neighbor knocked on the front door and asked me to watch a videotape."

Thankful for what she saw, Kathleen felt her prayers of making more than enough money for her family and controlling her own hours had been answered. Kathleen continues, "The video showed me that I could zero out my taxes in my house cleaning business and make great money as a TTP Independent Marketing Associate helping other single parents stay home.

"Even though we as single parents are extra busy, I know we have time to hand out videos that explain TTP's services and opportunity. People who watch a TTP video will realize that instead of working outside the home or a second job, they will have time to raise their children and still have plenty of money — a blessing for American families!"

She states from experience, "The pressure to pay bills is immediately removed because TTP customers effortlessly and legally increase their take-home pay on their next paychecks.

"I had worked at a real estate title company where I saw people refinancing their homes to pay off credit cards. The downside to refinancing is that it does not increase a person's monthly income. Even after re-financing, each month, families were falling short of the money they needed. So, they started using their credit cards again.

"It became a vicious cycle that often led to bankruptcy. Instead of refinancing or working away from their homes and children, people need to start home-based businesses to lower their taxes and immediately increase their incomes."

Another TTP customer, Bill Greenfield, helped a couple from Texas who were newlyweds with a baby on the way. Bill recounts the events: "The father was the only income earner in the family and grossed slightly over $1000 per month as a glass cutter. Needing desperately to increase his take-home pay, he spoke with our tax experts.

"Before he even joined as a customer, the experts helped him get an Advanced Earned Income Credit on his next paycheck. By starting his own home-based business he was able to zero out his taxes and the Advanced Earned Income Credit had the government actually paying him! He used the money to start his TTP business, purchase a good used car and provide for his wife and child. Through the course of events he was able to get a better job and he is doing great in the system now."

Bill assures us, "One of the things I've learned is that you make friends when you put food in their mouths or money in their pockets."

Irany and Pablo Didello agree and became TTP customers in February 1999. They like to make fun out of taxes at their special business meetings. Irany details, "We have banners saying 'Welcome to The Pay Raise Picnic!' We invite all the other TTP customers. We have other people stopping by asking how they can receive a pay raise, too. It is more inviting to attend a picnic versus a business meeting. Pablo and I want people to have fun on their way to financial freedom."

Irany was initially attracted to TTP because she wanted help with the taxes on the home-based businesses they had. She was uncertain of what deductions were safe and legal to take. Irany has found relief: "When I read about TTP's Tax Relief System, I bought it immediately. Now I have total access to unlimited tax advice and audit protection. The company guarantees that people can use the system for one year, and if they do not realize an additional $5,000 in deductions, the company refunds the money for the whole year."

Using TTP services was the answer to their daughter's prayers as Irany explains: "Our daughter, Fabiana, and son-in-law, Randy Campbell, were both working, but because of the high cost of California real estate, they couldn't afford their own home. They lived with us.

Wanting a home of their own, Fabiana decided to use the tax strategies recommended by The Tax People. The key strategy was to start a home-based business. The kids increased their write-offs which allowed them to increase their W-4 deductions.

"This gave them an immediate increase on their paychecks of $425 per month and allowed them to pay their credit cards. Five months into their TTP business, they were able to buy the house that they wanted."

Being immigrants, Irany talks about the biggest fear of people coming into the United States. "I was born in Brazil and Pablo in Uruguay, South America. Unfortunately, people who come to America from other countries have a lot of fears. They are confused that if they legally pay fewer taxes, the government will not give them their citizenship or their green card.

"People are joining The Tax People for reasons other than fear of the IRS. A 77-year-old gentleman in my organization became a TTP customer to stay actively involved with other people and keep his mind sharp. He didn't need the additional money but was very pleased when he followed The Tax People's system and saved $4,000 in taxes."

From experience, Irany reasons, "Most business opportunities require 90 days before they will pay you. The Tax People provides immediate increases on people's next paychecks plus daily, weekly and monthly compensation.

"The first 18 days of our TTP business, we received nine checks from the company. The people that have helped become customers are thanking us."

Upon meeting The Tax People's CEO Michael Cooper, Irany was immediately impressed: "Mike Cooper takes care of the Independent Marketing Associates. The compensation plan is very generous.

"I believe in the old saying 'Do unto others as you would want done unto you.' When Michael created the compensation plan, he decided that he would be paid by the exact same formula as the Independent Marketing Associates. This assures those of us in the field that if TTP changes the compensation plan, Michael Cooper's pay will also be modified. In the past two years, the compensation plan has become more and more lucrative. This is the way all CEO's should operate."

Friendship Is
Two Hearts Pulling One Load

Hank Oliveira became a customer of The Tax People in April 1998. He started and is succeeding in his TTP business with little formal education. He explains, "I don't have a good education. I've been out of school for years. Back then instead of learning, I played sports. I don't read very well, maybe at a third or fourth grade level. I'm self-taught in most everything I've done. The opportunities with The Tax People and my own desire to learn have made me smarter."

TTP has made Hank more aware of how the business world works. "I've gone from torn jeans and worn T-shirts to three piece suits. I love it. It inspires me every day."

Operating a small town taxi service doesn't produce much income for his family. He assures, "TTP is changing that. It is exciting and thrilling to know that there is a way out of the debt I'm in. There is a way to make life better for my family, a way to know financial freedom.

"I've tried for years to succeed. Not much has gone right. That's why I'm so thankful for Michael Cooper. See, Michael believed in me from the beginning. Even when I walked into his business meetings when I didn't own any good clothes to wear, Michael just looked past that and saw me for who I wanted to be. Michael Cooper is the first person in my life that believed in me. No one else, my father or my family, has ever thought I could make it. But Michael does."

Hank wrote Michael a note asking for his help learning how to succeed. Hank tells, "Michael helped me understand what TTP offers and how I could be a successful part. Now I know a lot about the company. So far, I've enrolled 10 Independent Marketing Associates and I'm earning money in my new business. This is the most success I've ever had. Soon, at a national convention, I will walk across the stage as a company leader."

Up until Hank joined The Tax People, he didn't own much. "The most expensive thing I've ever owned was a 24-carat gold Davie Allison commemorative rifle. I'm real proud of that collector rifle."

Hank explains, "I was so thankful that Michael believed in me, chose me as his friend and showed me how to succeed that I packed up my rifle and sent it to him. Every time he looks at it, I want him to remember how he takes the extra time to help people who others overlook or who may not understand how to succeed the first time.

"I will always keep going now that I know someone believes in me and truthfully wants me as part of the team. I am devoted to Michael and the company, and am now learning more about my own abilities."

Pastor Robert R. Chew, Ph. D. has witnessed the power of releasing people from the bondage of personal and financial hardships.

As the leader of the Zion Heal Baptist Church, Pastor Chew comments, "It is important for people to know all the information available to improve their lifestyles. The financial advantages derived from knowledge available to TTP customers can result in significant reward."

Through the power of information, Pastor Chew has been able to help congregation customers who were struggling financially. As he describes, "A single mother working for $10 an hour had three children attending elementary, junior high and high schools. Applying the tax principles from TTP, she generated an immediate take-home increase of $400 per month. In addition to having the money to catch up on her bills, after several years of walking she has now purchased a car."

The Tax People provides Pastor Chew with an additional tool to assist people in improving their lifestyles. "If you feed a person it is one meal. Teach them to fish and they can eat for a lifetime. This program provides an opportunity for people to enhance their lifestyles permanently.

"TTP is assisting people who would normally not have the resources or tax knowledge to help themselves in this way. Congress debates about tax cuts and who will receive them. The Tax People eliminates the entire debate because each individual can now determine to what degree they want to legally improve their tax situation. By accessing TTP's information you can immediately change your own tax situation. In a sense, you can receive the same big business tax breaks that the wealthy enjoy."

Pastor Chew feels that TTP allows people to determine their own financial destinies. "This whole year Congress has been talking about taxes and nothing has happened. For $300, a family can receive materials from The Tax People, set up the program and immediately reduce its tax burden."

In 1997, Thomas Silvio and his partners Kent McLaughlin and Mike Accurso started their TTP business.

Describing his situation, Tom says, "I was in the surplus business when Kent and Mike told me they had found a way to legally reduce their taxes. I was definitely looking for a way to cut my taxes legally."

Tom and his wife Annette became customers. Annette received a $450.00 pay raise the first month. The Tax People reviewed the Silvio's past tax returns and found Tom had overpaid his 1995 taxes by $3,600. The Tax People completed the paperwork and the IRS returned the money.

Next, Tom went to see his older sister Vita. He tells us, "I'm from a family of eight. Once I saw what The Tax People strategies did for me, I told my family. Vita is a single mom who was struggling financially. Upon becoming a customer, Vita increased her take-home pay by $500 per month. When The Tax People prepared her taxes for that year, Vita received an additional $5,000 refund. She was able to take her daughters, Anna, 16, and Carol Jo, 14, on a family vacation to Cancun."

Vita is currently building her own TTP business. On a part-time basis, she earns $1,000 per month over and above her tax savings. The additional income allows her to spend more time with her girls because Vita doesn't have to work overtime.

Anna and Carol Jo now attend private school. After school and homework, the girls work with Vita in the family business. The teens earn annual salaries of $4,250 each tax free, and Vita is able to deduct $8,500 from the business income.

For Tom and Annette, their lifetime dream was made possible by the income from their TTP business. Tom describes, "Annette and I believe that at least one parent should be home raising the children. Prior to TTP, Annette had to work outside the home two days a week. Our biggest dream came true the day that I told Annette our TTP business was earning enough money that she could stay home with Paul, Salvatore and Anthony. I don't cry but I can tell you that being able to provide Annette with the freedom to dedicate her time to raising our children made my eyes sweat. We hugged and kissed each other while thanking Michael Cooper for creating this opportunity."

The largest income from their TTP business was yet to come. When Annette was able to stay home with the children, that gave Tom additional hours. He and Annette agreed that time would be dedicated to building their business.

Two years into their TTP business, the Silvios have afforded a new home — double the size of their previous home. They also qualified for a new truck and Suburban for which The Tax People makes the payments.

Tom relates, "We haven't even scratched the surface. TTP has 20,000 customers from a pool of 120,000,000 taxpayers. I simply ask people if they want an immediate pay raise without asking their boss or working overtime. It sure is a lot easier to give people money than it is to take it from them."

Knowing The Tax People services span all income groups, Tom says, "Don't think 'This person is making a ton of money and wouldn't be interested.' People making $10,000 a year or $1,000,000 a year are all interested in cutting taxes. The more you make, the more you can deduct. Everyone wants to know how to take the deductions they are legally entitled to."

THE IRS IS GETTING FRIENDLIER

*"I had lost all my receipts and the
IRS agreed to let my tax return go as is."*

— **Art Hebner**, talking about the outcome
of a recent audit where he was
represented by The Tax People

The Tax People, America's taxpayer advocacy group, also referred to by some people as the "Taxbusters," is holding the IRS to its above claim.

On behalf of American taxpayers, The Tax People has become the equivalent of the "Tax Ghostbusters." The company and its CEO Michael Cooper have leveraged the experience and business networks of America's most powerful tax experts to protect and defend taxpayers. For Americans, the organization is curing one of the most common anxieties of life: fear of the IRS.

Norma Cruse used the services of The Tax People after she had IRS problems. Prior to joining as a customer of TTP, Mrs. Cruse and her husband mortgaged their home to pay a tax debt which the IRS claimed the couple owed.

"We received a notice from the IRS, took it to our accountant and ended up owing $10,000 in taxes, penalties and interest. We couldn't believe how helpless and frightened we felt. All we could do was borrow the money and pay-up."

Then the Cruses heard about The Tax People and joined, as Mrs. Cruse explains, "so we would never have to fight the IRS again." The Cruses used a free service offered by The Tax People where the Tax Dream Team, comprised of America's most powerful tax minds, reviews clients' past years tax returns for overpayments.

The couple sent The Tax People the same prior year's return of which the IRS claimed the Cruses owed $10,000 in back taxes. The Cruses were shocked to find the IRS actually owed them over $11,000! TTP completed the paperwork and the Cruses received their refund check.

Mrs. Cruse admits, "We really didn't believe it until we took the IRS check to the bank and it didn't bounce. It was legal and real. We just didn't know how to defend ourselves. So out of fear, we went into debt and struggled to pay the IRS when really, they owed us. This is the only recourse I know that Americans have. We overpaid for years because we were afraid of the IRS and ignorant of the laws. I don't fear the IRS any more."

Once the Cruses realized that their alliance with The Tax People had put the IRS in line, Mr. Cruse changed his W-4 and gave himself an instant $128 per week raise. Cautiously, he placed the money in a savings account in the event that at the end of the year they owed the IRS money. Instead, using the "Tax Relief System" from The Tax People and the guidance of the Tax Dream Team, the Cruses enjoyed an additional $2,300 refund.

Thomas W. Steelman, one of TTP's Tax Dream Team leaders, graduated from Southern Missouri State University with both B.S. and Masters degrees in business/accounting tax. He passed his CPA exam in 1978 as a revenue agent and was promoted through the highest ranks of the IRS until he chose to retire after 28 years. Now, Steelman is an enrolled agent. This allows him to represent and defend taxpayers in IRS situations without the individuals being present. TTP customers are greatly relieved to find that, when it comes to dealing with tax authorities like the IRS, Steelman and his colleagues can do all the talking and negotiating.

To this point, Steelman says, "We have won all cases involving taxpayers and the IRS. We expect to continue to do so."

A very bold statement considering TTP is inheriting whatever burdens the taxpayers bring along. Steelman continues, "Many times the records and returns of our new customers are in shambles. Often, new customers don't have records. Returns are a mess until the taxpayers get in here and learn the system. We have even had success with those hard-to-resolve cases between the IRS and taxpayers because the experts we have representing the taxpayers are extremely adequate counsel."

Surprisingly, Art Hebner, 74, had an overwhelmingly joyful outcome when dealing with the IRS. "I had lost all my receipts and the IRS agreed to let my tax return go as is." Hebner was referring to a recent audit where, previously, he had mistakenly burned his receipts thinking they were trash.

When Hebner opened his mailbox to find an audit notice from the IRS, he broke into a flu-like sweat. After he discovered the receipts he thought he had kept were gone, he nearly collapsed. How was he going to face the IRS and come out alive? Hebner had visions of his house being auctioned and his bank accounts being frozen. He had been in prior battles with the IRS and was wondering how much more he could take.

Hebner was already in the midst of his most recent audit when he joined The Tax People. Mr. Hebner's CPA, who was in the middle of touchy negotiations with the IRS, met with TTP's Tax Dream Team. The CPA advised Hebner to turn the entire audit procedure and negotiations over to The Tax People.

What was the result? The Tax Dream Team used the little-known 1929 Cohen Law and, even without receipts as proof of expenses, the IRS agreed to a "No Change" ruling. This decision gave Mr. Hebner two reasons to celebrate. First, it meant that Hebner's tax return stood as originally prepared. He didn't have to face his fears of losing his home or his bank accounts. Second, Mr.

Hebner slept well at night knowing that the IRS had agreed not to audit his next two years of returns.

As the National Director of Taxes for TTP's Tax Dream Team, Jesse Cota, a 33-year IRS veteran and retired IRS District Director of Southern California admits, "I am aware one of the biggest taxpayer fears is that the IRS will force people to sell their homes leaving families homeless, facing the streets."

Being a former IRS insider, Mr. Cota knows what the rest of us don't know: "The IRS has implemented a new procedure that any sale of a home has to be pre-approved by a district director. If selling the house would be disastrous to the family, (which it always is) the family could instead set up a payment plan which they could afford." Mr. Cota uses this, other IRS insider secrets and his strong network of current and former IRS executives and agents to the advantage of The Tax People customers whom he defends.

Mr. Steelman interjects, "Audit protection makes sure that if the government decides to abuse one of our customers, we step in and handle it properly. For the most part, taxpayers' fears are unfounded if the tax code is followed. The audit protection gives our customers the confidence that if they have made a mistake or are targeted for IRS abuse, they are covered."

Mr. Cota continues, "Over 99% of the time, we are able to resolve audits and issues and the taxpayer never has to personally meet with the IRS. Our Tax Dream Team works with the individuals to gather the correct information. Then, professionals from the Tax Dream Team communicate with the IRS. That is what ex-IRS people bring into the equation. We know the procedures that the IRS is required to follow. We use them to the taxpayers' benefit."

Marco Santos, Sr. had operated a taxi service in Mexico where he experienced severe financial setbacks when an accident damaged both his taxis beyond repair. Mr. Santos moved his family to the United States living in a tiny one-bedroom apartment looking for a way to repay his financial responsibilities in Mexico and continue to pay for his son's college education.

Mr. Santos' son Marco, Jr. talks about the family's experience: "It wasn't easy but my father, mother, sister Claudia and I were happy to be together. My father's goal is always to keep us safe, protected and together."

The elder Santo began operating a residential and commercial cleaning company. His son, Marco, inherited his father's entrepreneurial vision. In August 1998 Marco, Jr. and his wife, Blanca Garcia de Santos started a TTP business from home.

Mr. Santos and his wife, Marisela Reyes de Santos, were the first customers that the junior Santos enrolled. "Being a businessman, my father saw the benefits of the audit protection and the opportunity to make additional income for our family."

By March 1998, Mr. Santos, Sr. was too busy operating his growing residential and commercial cleaning business to build his TTP business. He considered canceling his TTP services.

The junior Santos stated, "I told my father that he needed the protection — even if I had to pay for it. My father was doing fine. We couldn't run the risk if he lost everything trying to fight an audit on his own."

Everyone in the Santos family was shocked when just a month later Mr. Santos, Sr. received an audit notice from the IRS.

Even though Mr. Santos believed he hadn't done anything wrong, he was once again dealing with the fear of losing everything. His mind filled with visions of revenue agents taking all his family owned.

The Santos immediately contacted TTP's Tax Dream Team. Tom Steelman was assigned to help the Santos family. Marcos, Jr. remembers, "My father sent the return that was being questioned to Mr. Steelman. All it took was a telephone call from the Tax Dream Team to the IRS auditor. Within two days, the audit was resolved over the phone without my father having to even talk to the IRS. Tom Steelman did a great job."

"My father was so happy that he had kept TTP's services. The expense of taking on the IRS could have wiped out our family — financially and emotionally. Being immigrants, the last thing we want to do is confront the United States government."

Marco, Jr. concluded, "Since then, the rest of my family who were skeptical have joined. My belief is now 1000%. I know TTP's service should be in the hands of all entrepreneurs who want to protect their businesses and their families."

Super Bowl Champion Helping Families Win

Pittsburgh Steelers Super Bowl Champion player Charles Davis knows first-hand the pain of dealing with the IRS. "Three years after I got out of the NFL, the IRS disallowed some of my deductions and put a tax lien on me. I knew what to do to win the Super Bowl, but I didn't know what to do to win against the IRS."

Davis tallies, "Back then, if I would have had experts to resolve this, I would have saved $20,000.

"Money is important. Not that you fall in love with it, but it is such a powerful tool. In my football days, there was so much I didn't know. When I was in the NFL, I would have loved to have saved more for my kids' college funds. Instead, I spent much of it by over-paying my taxes. I didn't realize I could put tax-free money aside for the kids."

Davis talks about his mission: "There are so many IRS-approved strategies available that I just have to let families across America know how much The Tax People can help them."

Taxpayers With
<u>Problems Find Peace</u>

When Tom Nash became a customer of The Tax People, he needed help. He had not filed tax returns for 5 years. "I had gotten involved with a group out of California espousing that you didn't have to file taxes because they were unconstitutional."

The IRS was closing in on him fast. According to the taxing authority, with penalties and interest, Tom owed them over $100,000 — an exorbitant sum for a man whose "mom-n-pop" business sold advertising on shopping carts. Tom felt trapped. "There's no way in a million years that I could pay that much money."

The IRS emptied his accounts and liened everything he owned. They sent letters to Tom's mother-in-law and clergyman. "I realized that I had made a mistake by believing I didn't have to file returns, but I had no idea how to make things right."

A friend told Tom how The Tax People were showing individuals how to legally save money on taxes and resolve tax problems — even serious ones.

"My wife Denise didn't want me getting involved in anymore 'tax deals.' She felt I had already done enough damage. But after we researched The Tax People, she gave it her blessing. That was the first time in 24 years that my wife has blessed any of my 'deals.'"

Nash's wife considers The Tax People the answer to her prayers. Tom adds, "We felt like we were running. I realized I had made a mistake, but how was I going to safely make amends?"

When Mr. Nash joined as a customer of The Tax People and informed them that he had not filed taxes in 5 years, the tax experts were glad that he had come to them.

According to Tom, The Tax People are conducting all communications with the IRS and making positive headway. The Nashes believe working with The Tax People is the most powerful option available to people who want to clean up their past and get back into the tax-paying system.

As Tom says with relief, "I feel at peace now and comfortable that the outcome will work out. For the first time in years, I'm not afraid."

Prior to joining The Tax People, Darrell and Maria Roberts had two major back-to-back business failures and a horrific tax situation.

Darrell admits, "We were financially drained. We were definitely going down for the count."

Maria listened to a tape about TTP's services called *Ex-IRS Agents Don't Lie*. The information on the tape instructed her to call The Tax People. The Roberts chose to immediately become customers. This gave them access to the Tax Dream Team who went on to resolve the IRS situation that the Roberts had felt was hopeless.

Darrell says with amazement, "We just didn't know how to get ourselves out of the problem we had with the IRS, but they (TTP) did. Even though our situation looked bad to us, the Tax Dream Team calmly, step-by-step put the answer together like a puzzle. They presented it to the IRS. We didn't even have to talk to the IRS."

TTP was able to secure a "No Change" ruling for the Roberts that meant they didn't owe the IRS any additional money. Mr. Roberts concludes, "You don't have to be a multi-millionaire to protect yourself and reduce your taxes; you just have to be affiliated with TTP."

Dan and Terri Cook had just started talking to people about their new TTP business when they approached a family friend who sold Mary Kay Cosmetics. Terri remembers, "She became very upset when we mentioned taxes. Then, she told us why. The IRS said our friend and her husband owed $6,000 in back taxes."

Terri expounds, "Our friend and her family were frantically trying to come up with $6,000 to get the IRS off their backs. Their fears were so great that they didn't even want to finish filing their current year taxes."

The Cooks recommended that their friend talk to TTP's Tax Dream Team who made a discovery that shocked Terri. On the returns that the IRS claimed her friend owned money, the friend hadn't taken all the deductions she legally could. The tax experts amended the woman's past tax returns. They not only legally wiped out the entire $6,000 tax debt but also generated a refund from the money she had over-paid during past years!

According to CEO Michael Cooper, "Most home business owners, and most other taxpayers, overpay their taxes by thousand of dollars each year. Big businesses with big tax firms write off 85% to 95% of their expenses. They pay taxes on their 5% to 15% net incomes. They can spend the rest.

"Small businesses and employees are afraid to take the legal deductions they are aware of, miss a bunch that they don't know, pay taxes on most of their income and try to survive on what's left. They are so afraid. Some have told me, 'I'd rather pay too much than have the IRS on my back.' This fear is due to having no real help available to 'average folks.' We're changing all that.

"We're teaching people that they don't have to fear our government. All we have to do is follow the law. The law is clear. You must pay every penny of tax you owe and not a single penny more. People should take the most aggressive legal stance and take every penny of deductions they can legally claim. Their fears cause many to only take half or less. In other words, to overpay their taxes by as much as 100%. This means that millions and millions of people are overpaying their taxes by thousands of dollars. Simple math means that we are overpaying our taxes by billions, which is just a drop in the bucket compared to the trillions collected.

"The government and the IRS only want what's legal. Yet many people are paying twice as much as they have to. We can equalize the playing field."

Ryan Vanderpool talks about a TTP customer who was in the midst of a 5-year audit when he became a client of The Tax People.

The man earned several million dollars a year in his own business. After the IRS conducted an audit, he was informed that they wanted $500,000.

With the financial resources to hire the best CPA's and tax attorneys that he could find, the man fought the IRS claim. The case was headed to federal court. The man was being deposed over the phone. Toward the end of the deposition, he was asked who his counsel was. The man replied that, in addition to his other counsel, The Tax People would also represent him.

Two days later, the IRS contacted him saying they chose to wipe out the debt. He didn't owe a thing.

Saving Families' Farms

In addition to entrepreneurs and families, tax professionals are discovering an alliance with The Tax People is beneficial. Elizabeth Crotts is a public accountant and tax professional in private practice. She is also an affiliate of The Tax People.

One of Mrs. Crott's many clients was an elderly woman who lived in a nursing home. Years prior, the woman had invested nearly all her money in a tax shelter and the fund's trustee stole the money. The elderly woman lost everything. She wasn't the only one. The media reported that this investment program was one of the largest senior citizens rip-offs in American history.

Elizabeth explains, "The IRS was fully aware of that thousands of senior citizens' retirement funds were stolen. Instead of realizing that this widow was alone, nearly penniless and barely existing on government subsidies, the IRS penalized her for the tax shelter not working. They were demanding over $100,000.

"My client had a small piece of property, the family farm, which she was preparing to sell to pay the IRS. This was her only asset. Turning it over to the IRS would have left her destitute. People at the IRS regional office were aware of her situation.

"The IRS continued to hound this poverty-stricken, little old lady and wanted $14,000 immediately. This woman was lucky if she had $14 for clothes let alone an extra $14,000. But the IRS wouldn't let up. The fear and stress were taking their toll on her already fragile health. The IRS didn't seem to care. They only wanted her money."

Elizabeth knew how to legally remedy the elderly woman's problem, but she didn't have the clout nor connections within the IRS to resolve it. Mrs. Crotts felt that she was getting nowhere working on a regional level.

She recalls, "I asked TTP's Tax Dream Team if they could help this elderly woman find some peace and protection from the IRS. One of the Tax Dream Team members had an already scheduled meeting at IRS headquarters in Ogden, Utah. During the course of business, he discussed this woman's case and presented the documentation, rulings and previous case histories I had assembled.

"The entire case was immediately dismissed based on the information gathered. The woman kept her farm and what little money she had to pay for her nursing home expenses. Thank God for The Tax People and its Tax Dream Team! Even though, as a CPA and tax professional, I had the knowledge of what was necessary to have the case dismissed, I needed The Tax People on my side to reach the result."

Unlike Elizabeth Crotts, Bill Fox was not a tax expert. But, as a customer of The Tax People he knew where turn to for help.

Bill knew a woman who owned a farm on which the IRS had filed a lien. He tells, "The family thought that life as they knew it was finished. Every morning they woke up, looked outside and expected the IRS to drive up and seize their home. The stress had become unbearable."

TTP's Tax Dream Team, headed by Jesse Cota, intervened and represented the family in negotiations with the IRS. The tax lien on the farm was immediately removed.

Bill continues, "I was thrilled. The woman broke down and cried. She kept her family farm because I showed her where to turn for help."

An Audit Gone Good

A customer since February 1999, Kathy Coover tells the story of her friend Larry who had also joined: "He received a notice from the IRS that he was going to be audited. Larry called The Tax People right away. The IRS was questioning his return for about $3,000. He was afraid with penalties and interest that amount would snowball."

Kathy proceeds, "TTP's Tax Dream Team handled the audit while Larry went on with his life. Out-of-the-blue, the Tax Dream Team called Larry and told him that a $600 refund was on its way to Larry from the IRS!"

Kathy admits with a smile, "Larry joked he hoped that he'd get audited again."

Tax Issues Resolved Quickly

Thirty-eight-year-old GJ Reynolds discovered how quickly tax issues can be resolved with the right players in the game.

GJ explains his situation: "Four years I had been fighting the IRS. They liened my property saying I owed over $60,000. I didn't believe I owed it, but fighting the IRS alone is an uphill battle. It comes down to how much time, money and energy a person is willing to spend. Fight solo and you'd better be prepared to spend a lot. Even if you have money on your side, the odds are against you in a game where few people know the rules."

GJ joined The Tax People and told the tax experts about his situation. "For a couple of years I hadn't filed returns. For 1994, the IRS filed one for me."

The IRS said GJ owed $27,000 for that year alone and $60,000 in total.

TTP's Tax Dream Team informed GJ that by using what information he could provide, they would complete and file all three years of back returns including 1994. Even though his information was accurate, GJ thought the chance was slim that IRS would accept the returns and the deductions.

GJ recounts the story: "In just six months, my four year battle on my 1994 return came to an end. The Tax Dream Team took my $27,000 tax debt and working with the IRS reduced it to $1,000. The Tax People saved me $26,000. Once the Tax Dream Team took over, I didn't have to talk to the IRS. They handled everything."

Thumbs-Up From
Assistant Attorney General

Mrs. Smith, a former Missouri Assistant Attorney General for six years, currently operates her own growing private legal practice. She looked over TTP's services with her clients in mind and decided to join as a customer, herself. Mrs. Smith confirms, "I have several hundred clients sleeping better at night. Once we got the fear of tax deductions, returns and audits out of their lives, they became better business people — more creative. They became better moms and dads because many of their fears and money worries were gone. If a person has money worries, they can't do anything else. It stifles their creativity and initiative."

Mrs. Smith informs, "There is no place I know of that has this kind of protection and information. There is no course in high school that teaches this. There's no course in college or law school that teaches the unreadable tax code boiled-down to 52 simple-to-understand pages. In addition, you receive audit protection, tax preparation and the network of experts who you can personally call and rely on."

Judy Fletcher, a retired income tax professional who prepared thousands of returns over her 20-year career, personally experienced TTP services when she sent them two years of her own meticulously prepared tax returns. The amendments TTP's Tax Dream Team recommended resulted in a $3750 refund for Ms. Fletcher. "That was money that I had left on the table. I was shocked," declared Fletcher.

Ms. Fletcher reviewed the tax relief system, "I immediately saw how this was going to save people a load of time. There had never been anything mapped out for people with home-based businesses on what to do for their taxes. I wanted the information for my personal use and it was by accident that I started working the business. I told my friends about the audit protection and tax expertise, they wanted it."

From her professional experience, Ms. Fletcher claims many tax professionals advise their clients against taking numerous deductions when completing tax returns. She reasoned, "The professionals know that if their clients are audited, the professional will spend too much time learning how to defend the audit. People need to find tax experts who understand audit procedures and are highly educated on the current laws and processes." Fletcher added, "With TTP, you have full audit protection from the tax dream team. Who better knows what the IRS is looking for and how to work with them than former IRS employees?"

TTP customers Denny and Darlene Mundell report the results of their TTP business: "People are quickly enrolling for TTP's services. As a result of offering instant pay raises, 90% of the people we talk to sign up."

Denny talks about the work and the rewards: "We dedicate one hour a day, six days a week to our TTP business. October 1999 our bonus checks totaled over $8,000 for the month."

Those 6 hours a week paid off in multiples. For two months over the summer, the Mundells decided to travel on vacation and their TTP bonus continued to travel to their mailbox. Together they shout, "It's mailbox magic!"

TAX BUSTERS
MAKE IRS PAY YOU

"In reality, many of these taxpayers are and have been overpaying their taxes by 30 % and more."

— **Scott Turner,** tax expert for a legal firm with 5.2 million clients, talking about taxpayers ***not*** using the services of TTP tax preparers

While The Tax People provide tax saving strategies and guidance, its national network of affiliated tax professionals prepare customers' income taxes, amended returns and accounting work. Customers are comforted by knowing that the selected professionals complete a tax training program administered by The Tax People and prepare returns according to TTP's *Tax Relief System.* Tax professionals are thrilled by the immediate and positive effect on their firms' bottom-lines caused by the large number of new clients that TTP can refer.

Once tax professionals have completed their training, they are referred to as "affiliates." During the last three months of 1999, over 500 affiliate offices were approved and services made available to customers. By the end of the year 2000, TTP estimates they will have an affiliated tax professional network of over 2,000 offices.

The affiliates are CPA's, enrolled agents, tax attorneys and other tax professionals who are signing contracts with TTP to provide tax services and preparation of customers' returns according to TTP's tax strategies.

What You Can Do To
Save Money On Your Taxes

CEO Cooper elaborates, "Our customers are no longer willing to go to unenlightened tax preparers that simply fill in the forms. They insist on professionals who know how to maximize home-based business strategies to the benefit of taxpayers who want to legally keep thousands of dollars every year in their pockets."

Assembling TTP's network of professionals required great skill. Michael Cooper explains, "When the idea for The Tax People first came to the surface, Vice President Todd Strand took it to heart. Within days he developed and implemented a plan to assemble America's most powerful tax professionals all on one team."

Michael continues, "Todd is an incredible and highly talented person. He is able to accomplish a great deal with lightening speed. It is because of Todd that we have the Tax Dream Team which is our network of in-house experts, affiliated professionals and well-connected tax authorities."

Tax Professionals
Watch Their Incomes Soar

Tax professionals are very interested in being associated with The Tax People. Michael elaborates, "We send tax professionals hundreds of new clients. We can double tax firms' revenues by sending them new business totaling over $100,000 or $200,000 per year, per firm."

As a CPA for 20 years, Scott Turner, the tax expert for a legal firm with 5.2 million clients, describes the benefit of being affiliated with TTP: "Conservatively, TTP will increase my cash flow by $250,000 this year. I could increase my business even more depending on how well I can handle the growth. I will help as many of these new clients as I can. Those that I can not, I will refer to other TTP affiliates."

Mr. Turner continues, "I believe that The Tax People will surpass the size of H & R Block and Jackson-Hewitt. The biggest difference between The Tax People's tax affiliate experts and other firms' tax preparers is year-round tax planning. H & R Block trains its employees to prepare returns according to information provided by the clients. They do not typically volunteer on-going tax planning.

"I see a niche in the market for tax experts to provide the tax strategies clients deserve and prepare their returns for reasonable fees. It used to be that in order for people to receive the advice and services at the quality of TTP, they had to pay very high prices."

Turner remarks, "TTP helps people and families find freedom from tax burdens by placing an extra $300 to $400 dollars into their pockets each month. Every recommended deduction is 100% legal as it is applied to each individual's situation. Clients have unlimited access to the Tax Dream Team that provides customers with the guidance needed to decide which deductions work for their particular situations."

Pro-Taxpayer Professionals

Jesse A. Cota is National Director of Taxes for The Tax People's Tax Dream Team. As a 33-year IRS veteran and retired IRS District Director of Southern California, he brings his extensive knowledge to TTP customers.

Jesse confirms, "My first responsibility is to verify the legal basis for all tax strategies being developed for recommendation to our customers.

"TTP is not a tax protester group. Rather, our tax philosophy is that people need to be aggressive with their tax returns and take the deductions to which they are legally entitled. We also know that, without our help, sometimes people become so aggressive that they mistakenly take deductions that they should not be taking.

"There is a fine line between legal tax avoidance and harmful tax evasion. We position for the most aggressive posture we can in such a way that if an audit occurs, everything will work out fine."

TTP's *Tax Relief System* is footnoted to the IRS Tax Code and Regulations. While it produces incredible tax savings for clients, it has already withstood the scrutiny of the IRS. Mr. Cota confirms, "The IRS has already reviewed tax returns completed according to our *Tax Relief System* and has agreed returns completed according to our system are within tax law."

The Tax People's mission is to work with its clients to present the best tax posture possible through proper tax planning and correct advice. Mr. Cota explains, "Every tax professional involved with TTP is a client advocate. Because many of us are former IRS people, at first, new customers may assume we are pro-IRS. We are not pro-IRS. We are pro-client. Pro-client means protecting and shielding our customers. This can mean telling clients they are not able to take certain deductions according to the tax laws, but we work with them to find other deductions that they can take to come out even better.

"Another part of our job is that if customers are audited by the IRS or any state taxing agency, we represent them at no additional charge. This means we protect our customers even if we have not completed the tax returns ourselves or the returns were completed before clients became customers. As tax professionals and experts, we act on behalf of our clients."

The Tax People and Jesse Cota have assembled an impressive team of experts. Mr. Cota explains, "Few taxpayer advocacy organizations as effective as The Tax People exist because there are only so many former IRS employees. It is a finite pool to draw from. I don't know of any other taxpayer organization that could pull together this type of expertise. I am not aware of any other company offering our level of services, protection and results."

To access the Tax Dream Team, customers can use various methods and receive prompt answers to their questions. Jesse directs, "In 52 easy-to-follow pages, the *Tax Relief System* clarifies immediate tax deductions available to home-based business owners. It includes an eight-set audiotape program and easy fill-in-the-blank documentation. We also offer one-on-one consulting via hundreds of affiliated offices nationwide. Clients also have access through e-mail, fax and on-going live, interactive conference calls at all times of the day and night.

"We tell people that we are here to help. In addition to tax saving strategies, we help people who have not filed returns to get back into the system. We welcome them with open arms. Our goal is to help taxpayers come into compliance with the IRS in a way that is advantageous for the taxpayers and the government.

"When people who have not filed tax returns come to us for help, we don't place blame. Rather, we look for solutions. Some TTP customers have tax issues. They may owe the state or the IRS money. They may have collection or audit problems."

Mr. Cota continues, "We deal with the IRS by trying to arrive at a solution that will benefit our clients. If the tax laws are such that our customers owe a tax authority, we negotiate to arrange a reduced payment plan. When penalties and interest are involved, in some instances we can have those removed.

"People come to us because we are a safe place. People want to resolve tax situations and move forward without the threat of the IRS."

Jesse says with concern, "The family unit can find itself threatened because of tax problems. A husband and wife owe the IRS a large sum of money and one blames the other. One spouse may be telling the other to resolve the situation or face divorce. Part of that is because the IRS is putting liens on their properties, garnishing their wages or taking other actions that by law they can do if taxpayers don't make arrangements. Most people in this situation don't know what they can do to resolve these problems.

"The unfortunate part is that when people receive a notice from the IRS, many don't respond. They are afraid. We tell them to bring the situation to our attention. We can help them. We are former IRS agents who know the procedures necessary to resolve problems.

Ninety-nine percent of the time, our clients don't even have to talk to the IRS. We are a protective shield of knowledge and experience. We are the point of contact and communication.

"In addition to communicating with the IRS, we talk with the spouses and help them outline a plan to resolve the IRS matter. This may prevent couples from splitting up. The family unit can become stronger.

"The one thing that is most important to our company and to CEO Mike Cooper is families. I feel so good that we can work out people's problems with the IRS. Our top goal is to maintain family units. We help them live more peacefully and prosperously on a day-by-day basis than before they were associated with The Tax People."

People become a part of TTP because the company goes out of its way to help clients. Jesse verifies, "We are a company that people can put their faith in. We are a company that stands behind its word and does exactly what we say."

Enrolled Agent Matt Briseno joined TTP June 1, 1999. He tells why: "What most impressed me about The Tax People was Jesse Cota and the team of experts who head up the Tax Dream Team. They are well-versed, well-connected and very powerful when it comes to understanding, applying and defending legal tax-saving strategies."

Matt was also impressed to find that for tax professionals like him, the training offered by The Tax

People qualified for continuing education credits. He states, "That meant the tax-strategies had been approved and were legal."

The number one question most tax professionals receive from their clients is, "What can I do to save money on my taxes?"

Matt says with relief, "Finally, I have something to guide them step-by-step that provides measurable tax saving results. I don't need to educate clients individually. The Tax People completes the education process. By being a TTP affiliate, I receive tons of new client referrals. I have piles of amendments to complete. Customers are coming to me to have their taxes prepared."

Enrolled Agent Gene Franklin heads his family's CPA firm that was started in 1940. The firm became a TTP affiliated office in October 1999.

After being in the industry 35 years, Gene explains why he chose to be a TTP affiliate: "Tax professionals are paid to complete customers' taxes according to TTP's tax system. The system is footnoted directly to the IRS code and regulations. Everything is black and white. As serious professionals, The Tax People administer tax strategies for customers according to what law allows. Then, TTP's in-house tax experts offer complete audit protection for their customers. The Tax Dream Team is mostly comprised of former IRS agents with an average of 30 years experience each. They are powerful tax professionals who defend the customers."

Gene explains an additional reason for becoming a TTP affiliate: "The first 2½ months as a TTP affiliate my firm increased by 150 new fee-paying clients. During 2000, I am expecting between 500 and 1,500 new clients."

According to a recent article in the *Wall Street Journal*, there are 120,000,000 taxpayers in America. Gene comments, "I believe The Tax People will experience 20% market penetration."

That would compute to 24,000,000 taxpayers as customers of The Tax People. Those TTP customers will require tax preparation, accounting, payroll services from the tax professionals who are TTP affiliates.

Tax Professional affiliates have the option of working as Independent Marketing Associates in addition to preparing customers' tax returns.

Gene continues, "I have looked at hundreds of network marketing opportunities. Everything else is a variation of the pills-and-potions or discount programs. Sooner or later we all get tired of the better vitamin or biggest Internet shopping club. The Tax People services free up cash, and cash never goes out of style. Combine that with the zeal that people have to legally not pay taxes. When you save them significant money, they are overjoyed."

The *Tax Relief System* has passed the test as Gene states, "Thousands of tax professionals nationwide have endorsed the *Tax Relief System*. This shows that the deductions are quite legal. Then, TTP has backed-up their system with America's most powerful tax strategists and defenders.

"If tax professionals and CPA's don't learn and use these tax saving techniques, they will lose clients who will become increasingly angry at overpaying their taxes."

Why Tax Professionals
Are Becoming TTP Affiliates

Lora Lee Manikam is the Director of Affiliated Tax Professionals for The Tax People. She explains, "We have invited tax professionals nationwide to become affiliated with our company. We are referring our Independent Marketing Associates and their prospects to the tax professionals' places of business. The professionals prepare customers' income taxes, amended returns and accounting work."

Lora Lee understands day-to-day tax firm operations: "Prior to The Tax People, I was with H & R Block where I worked my way up the ranks to assistant district manager. I managed the largest district in Kansas City right next to the world headquarters, supervising several office locations."

Clarifying why she chose to work for The Tax People, "I believe in what TTP is doing for families across the nation. The tax-saving strategies are solid and outlined fully in the United States Tax Code and Regulations. I am impressed with the in-house tax team we have assembled. The Tax People's service has mass appeal to American families. We help thousands of working Americans legally save money on their taxes and put hundreds of dollars a month back into their pockets instantly."

Lora Lee reveals the difference between the services of The Tax People and other leading tax preparation firms: "Our tax professionals actually help individuals implement the advanced, tax-saving strategies that we recommend. Few tax preparers outside of TTP are even aware of these strategies. If they are, they are not sure what steps are needed to implement them. For example, the tax-saving strategies of hiring your children or creating a medical reimbursement plan. These leave most tax professionals puzzled.

"H & R Block tax preparers are no different. Normally, when you have your taxes completed by H & R Block, you supply them with all of your records. They prepare your tax return based on the information you give them. They do not research or assist you with implementing tax-saving strategies. The most they may do is suggest a simple strategy that you have overlooked like deducting your home mortgage interest."

Lora Lee compares, "The difference between H & R Block and our company is that clients can contact our in-house Tax Dream Team for customized tax-saving strategies and how to implement these strategies to maximize their deductions. The Tax People helps clients plan their taxes to receive the maximum deduction to the extent allowed by law.

"Accountants who own small professional practices are faced with the challenge of building their businesses. We assist tax professionals to increase their businesses by hundreds of clients a month and thousands of dollars a year. Many accounting firms are hungry for year-round business. They are spending money marketing and advertising with no guarantee of results. We offer select tax professionals a unique situation. We have thousands of customers who are actively seeking tax professionals to implement our recommended tax-saving strategies and prepare tax returns.

"Our customers have been introduced to new home-based businesses. They are looking for the preparation services of competent tax preparers. Professionals can receive thousands of new fee-paying clients. The payment for services is made directly from the customer to the tax professional."

Lora Lee states, "Due to our massive on-going growth and demand for these services, I can never see a time that we will have too many tax professionals."

When approaching a tax professional about the opportunity to be a TTP affiliate, what does a person say? Lora Lee directs, "When initiating conversations with tax professionals ask, 'Is your firm looking to drastically increase its revenues by thousands and thousands of dollars? Are you wanting to join a large company that can send you hundreds and hundreds of clients per month?' If the answer is yes, then I suggest that the tax professional call and listen to our Tax Professional

Conference Call. In 60-minutes this live, interactive phone meeting explains our affiliate program and provides time for questions and answers."

Listening in on the specialized Tax Professional Conference Call held several times each week convinced tax firm owner Robert Golledge to become a TTP tax affiliate.

He tells why he is glad that he did: "We have had a 35% increase in our business because of our association with The Tax People. That is quite a bit of business for us. I would venture to say that we will be doing 1,200 tax returns next year. We will be adding additional preparers for our next tax season.

"As an affiliate of The Tax People, it is an added benefit to have TTP's in-house tax professionals handle audits. They are former IRS agents and know exactly what the tax laws allow."

Robert continues, "Without an ongoing relationship with the IRS like TTP has, to succeed in audits, a professional has to be confrontational. I just like to be the nice guy. When this program came along, it even removed the burden of audits off my back as the professional tax preparer.

"My lifestyle has changed since my affiliation with The Tax People. My goal is to work three days a week. My wife and I have been married 20 years. We have 5 sons from 4 to 15-years-old. Right now is a prime time for me to spend at home with the boys. I'm hiring additional professionals for the firm and taking more of a managerial role.

"Where in the world would independent tax firms be able to experience this degree of growth? It has been wonderful for us. The Tax People's goal is to have neighborhood affiliate offices in every city in the United States."

Robert reasons, "H & R Block completed over 40,000,000 tax returns last year. They didn't offer tax-saving strategies. They are just a tax service. The Tax People is the fastest growing tax consulting firm in the United States right now. I think there will come a time that we will be bigger than H & R Block. People receive more service for their buck from us."

Talking about the legality of TTP's tax strategies Robert says, "The tax code and regulations are what they are. TTP's recommended deductions are from the tax code and regulations. The Tax People were smart enough to create a program incorporating all these legal deductions and make it easy for the average American to understand. That is what people want. People hear about all these deductions and want to know how they can save money, too."

Tax professionals around America are agreeing that owning and operating home-based businesses is the last great money-saving strategy left for taxpayers.

Tax expert Frankie Ruth whose firm was one of the first TTP affiliates confirms, "As tax professionals, we could recommend the home-based businesses strategy to our clients, but we didn't have anything tangible to offer clients. The Tax People is our answer. Now, when we inform clients about tax-saving strategies and they want to take control of their taxes, we can offer them a complete package. Clients want immediate take-home pay raises, a legitimate home-based business, legal tax strategies and complete audit protection."

Frankie talks about the results of being an affiliate: "Prior, as the owner of an independent tax preparation firm, I knew my company's future growth would have been one client at a time.

"Within my first year as an affiliate, my practice doubled its volume. For my practice to grow to that degree, without TTP, would have required at least five years of effort.

"In the second year as an affiliate, my revenues doubled again. My profit margins have been extremely healthy during this explosive growth. I have spent zero dollars on advertising to expand my tax and accounting practice. There is nothing in our industry that can do this. I've had to expand my staff to four people to handle our expanding client load."

Affiliates can receive new clients who have already been educated by the *Tax Relief System.* This pleases Frankie. "Before TTP, my method was to educate each client individually, but many were not positioned to pay for professional tax expertise by the hour. Even if clients could afford the expertise, I could only help one person at a time."

In addition to the need for client education, there is another reason Frankie is happy with TTP. "A large number of people haven't paid taxes for years. These people would like to set things right. They feel the situation is too far-gone and don't know what to do. Then fear sets in. TTP is successfully helping people clean-up current and past tax issues.

"New lives are created when tax debts are brought under control and money is once again available. Lack of money can wreck marriages quicker than anything else I've seen. This opportunity has saved and repaired marriages by giving families instant pay raises and steering others from bankruptcy."

Frankie comments on her own situation: "I saw my family being torn apart because we worked, worked and worked. My husband was an ironworker and because of The Tax People he has been able to retire. Now we earn money together, eat together and send our son, Tyler, to school together."

Tyler works in the family business and Frankie has found it to be a tremendous parenting tool: "Through entrepreneurship parents can teach the concept of money and that the ATM is not a glorious machine that spits out cash as kids approach. Tyler knows that an exchange of value happens to receive money. For Tyler that exchange is sending faxes, e-mails and packages.

"This business gives children great self-esteem. I could not have provided this type of self-esteem for Tyler with any other tool. We don't have to tell him to go play when we are busy. He can sit right there with us and help. Tyler's concept of business and taxes is healthy."

People of all ages are experiencing significant benefits from being associated with The Tax People.

Tax professional and enrolled agent, Jim Edwards has been an affiliate of The Tax People since April 1998.

Jim speaks about his experiences as a tax professional: "People want help with taxes but they don't know where to go or whom to trust. The Tax People is the place to turn. As more and more of the American public discovers this, we are going to have a tremendous influx of people coming for tax and accounting services. I think being involved with The Tax People is the best move a tax professional could make."

He describes the relationship: "As a CPA and owner of a small accounting firm, being an affiliate of The Tax People has had an astronomical effect on my business. As of the end of October 1998, my total tax work for that month was $70.00. As of October 15, 1999 it was $4,983.00.

"My revenue was seasonal because a majority of my business was between November and April. For the other six months, business came to a stand-still with just small revenues from payroll and accounting services. Since becoming a TTP affiliate, I have clients all over the

United States that TTP refers to me. I spent zero advertising dollars to increase my earnings 7,118%."

Jim continues, "Now my firm does more than tax returns during tax season. We do enormous numbers of amended tax returns. I no longer depend just on the business in my own community; I now have clients from Florida to New York to New Jersey to California to Kansas."

D. Max Ritz is an enrolled agent and became a TTP affiliate in September 1999.

Ms. Ritz explains, "Without advertising efforts on my part, TTP refers people to my firm at no cost to me. I offer a real down-home, one-on-one service to all my clients. I want to take care of everybody. TTP customers work directly with me and they receive total audit protection through The Tax People.

"Being a TTP affiliate is great because I can take on as many clients as I want. When I want more, The Tax People refers them almost instantaneously. The Tax People has referred clients to me from all areas of the USA."

She states, "In any small tax and accounting practice there are slow times. Since being a TTP affiliate, I am able to put food on my table without worrying. It's been a financial blessing. No matter what time of the year new TTP customers enroll, affiliate tax professionals are very busy with customers' amended returns. The fees are great money for preparers that we normally would not have."

Max adds, "It is a great feeling to find deductions that were missed and give TTP customers their money back from the IRS and state agencies.

"I expect TTP to give H & R Block continued competition for tax preparation. The Tax People proactively plan to save individuals money on their taxes. H & R Block and even conservative CPA's have no reason to help clients save money. They make their money from filling out tax forms from the information clients provide. The Tax People lets customers know all their tax-saving options and then helps customers implement."

For deductions, most Americans have home mortgage interest, real estate taxes, charitable contributions, children and IRA's. Deductions run out fast. When people have home-based businesses they are able to convert personal expenses into tax deductible expenses. As a result of taxpayers understanding and implementing these strategies, TTP affiliates have a steady flow of new clients.

CPA Thomas McGraw became involved with The Tax People September 1999 as he explains, "During January 2000, TTP referred 125 clients to my firm. I feel this tax season my business will grow by an additional 250 to 500 clients.

Thomas continues, "There are three major preparers in the USA: The Tax People, H & R Block and Jackson Hewitt. At Block and Hewitt, you walk through the door and have your tax forms completed.

"At TTP, tax professionals strategize your taxes with you all year and then a tax expert completes your taxes for you."

The Tax People offers additional services for taxpayers who need more than tax-saving strategies.

If you read the *New York Times* or turned on the TV to watch *Good Morning, America*, you could have the opportunity to see nationally renowned tax expert Steve Kassel. Mr. Kassel's professional firm is devoted exclusively to representing taxpayers that owe the IRS or state agencies over $100,000. Because Steve is one of five leading tax experts in America, the media regularly turns to him for comment on both taxpayer and IRS behaviors.

Steve was an IRS revenue officer from 1987 to 1992. He saw a need for taxpayers to have someone communicate on their behalf with the IRS. Steve explains, "I left to start my own business irstaxes.com. In 1997, the United States government flew me to Washington, D.C. to testify before The National Committee on IRS Restructuring that was researching the collection methods being implemented by the IRS. The committee's recommendations form the framework for the historical IRS Reform Bill signed by President Clinton in 1998."

Steve talks about his affiliation with The Tax People: "The first thing that caught my attention was the guarantee that TTP was offering. If taxpayers followed TTP's *Tax Relief System* and during the first year did not receive $5,000 in additional tax deductions, the company would refund the taxpayers' money. I wondered how they could make that guarantee.

"The more I read about TTP's services, the more I realized what they were offering was legitimate, legal, moral and ethical. I was surprised someone hadn't thought of offering those services before."

Mr. Kassel went on to discover that The Tax People provides clients with legal methods to reduce their tax liabilities, as well as solve problems.

One of those avenues has become Mr. Kassel's weekly conference call where Tax People customers who feel they might have major tax problems can call, ask question and receive answers.

Steve understands the challenges that face people who find themselves substantially indebted to the IRS: "Often, the general public does not understand how people can owe $100,000 or more taxes. The way it typically starts is that self-employed people forego making their estimated quarterly tax payments.

"April arrives and these taxpayers realize they haven't paid taxes for the previous year. They figure if they don't file a return, the IRS won't realize. That often works for a period of time. The IRS doesn't know you have a problem until you file the return."

Steve continues, "By not filing, taxpayers incur an additional penalty of up to 25% of the taxes due. People can very easily owe $15,000 in taxes each year. Avoid filing and they easily owe $25,000 in penalties and interest. The next year the same thing occurs. The IRS knocks on their doors, sends letters or files returns for the taxpayers. People can very easily owe $100,000 if four years go by."

Steve Kassel talks about an option available to taxpayers who are being pursued by the IRS for large tax debts: "Our goal is to do an 'Offer and Compromise.' We go to the IRS with hat-in-hand to tell them that the taxpayers don't have the money to pay the tax in full. The IRS uses a mathematical equation to determine what they will accept from taxpayers negotiating settlements.

"The basic two-part equation is whatever you can afford to pay them on a monthly basis multiplied by 48 months. This is strictly figured from the taxpayers' incomes minus their living expenses. The second half is the value of assets. The IRS deducts 20% off the fair market value of taxpayers' assets and adds that to the amount they can afford to pay."

Mr. Kassel reveals, "Nationwide, a typical offer amount is approximately 15-16% of the total amount due. My offer is typically 10-11% because my clients owe more than the national average."

A great deal of expertise is needed to keep on top of both problem resolution and the latest tax strategies.

The Shocking Truth Revealed

Dave Dalton has been an enrolled agent for 22 years and sits on the Board of Directors for the California Society of Accounting and Tax Professionals.

Mr. Dalton discloses, "Most people are shocked to discover what little taxation expertise is needed for CPA's and attorneys to be licensed. Both the California Bar Exam for attorneys and the Certified Public Accountant Exam are 3 days, 8 hours each day for a total of 24 hours of examination. Only 2 hours which is less than 10% of either exam are on taxation."

Mr. Dalton explains the requirements for an enrolled agent: "There are two options for becoming enrolled agents. If people survive as IRS agents for over 5 years without being fired, they receive an Enrolled Agent card as they leave. The other option is a 2-day, 16-hour test developed and administered by the IRS. It is focused strictly on taxation. If people have the experience and can pass the test, they become enrolled agents. It was the most grueling exam I've ever taken in my life."

The certification of Enrolled Agent allows professionals to represent clients in front of the government without the clients present.

Mr. Dalton has extensive experience defending clients in front of state and federal taxing agencies. In 1985, he decided to expand his tax practice and purchase another. After the purchase and to his surprise, he discovered his newly acquired practice had over 7,000 pending federal and state audits that required years of his attention. In addition, he has handled over 1,000 tax appeals, 350 tax court cases and over 500 collection cases. All of these have been resolved to his clients' benefits.

Mr. Dalton talks about how he became involved with The Tax People: "I was approached by Jesse Cota who asked me to become a TTP affiliate. From his years in the IRS, he knew that my firm was very skilled and that I played hard ball when it came to the IRS."

An IRS District Director once told Mr. Dalton, "My people don't like to work with you because you make them go through a lot of hoops to collect their money."

Knowing his background, The Tax People asked David to review the *Tax Relief System.* Mr. Dalton states, "The quality and legality of the *Tax Relief System* and recommended deductions are 100% correct. I believe in the good that this company is doing for taxpayers."

In just the first *three months* that Mr. Dalton and his two firms became affiliates, TTP has sent over 240 local and 40 mail-in clients to his office. "I expect to double my business this year. I won't have to increase my advertising budget to get these clients into my door. It's easy to understand why I am very grateful to The Tax People."

THE TAX PEOPLE PHENOMENON

"This is an awesome responsibility."
— **Michael Cooper,** CEO,
Renaissance TTP, Inc.,
The Tax People

On September 28, 1999, the *Wall Street Journal* reported that families and spouses are playing a bigger role in many former "corporate" issues, such as determining which executives people choose to follow. "Potential clients want to meet executives' spouses 35% to 50% of the time. Five years ago, the issue never came up."

Most people would agree that if you want to get to know people with whom you're thinking of building relationships, whether personal or business, spend time with their families.

You may be reading this book while considering whether to use The Tax People's services. You may be deciding to become an Independent Marketing Associate. During this process, you may want the opportunity to participate in the same ritual as the folks on Wall Street.

When people meet each other for the first time they naturally engage in a "getting-to-know-you" ritual. Many of The Tax People's Independent Marketing Associates are pleased and even more excited about this company's future after they meet with Mary Cooper, wife of CEO Michael Cooper, and a truly enjoyable person.

Mary Cooper waited until the age of 38 to return to college and earn her Masters Degree in social work. Spend any amount of time with her and you will know that she is blessed with a great mind and a heart of gold. She smiles humility — a rare trait during mass success.

Mary is the Chief Operating Officer of the most important aspect of the Coopers' lives, their family: four children — two grown and two at home. One glance will confirm that they are an energetic, all-American bunch.

Just ask this proud mother and wife about her family and her words emanate from a confident smile. About her husband, Mary answers, "When I think of Mike, I think of optimism. Mike endured the very tragic loss of his first wife when he was just a 25-year-old father with two toddlers ages 1 and 3-years-old.

"There are times when those of us who have suffered tragic loss give up or never hope again. Mike kept his optimism and believed in the power of love."

Seventeen years later, Mike also endured the tragic loss of his best friend, sidekick, and business partner, Johnny Meadows. Johnny and Mike worked side-by-side even when they were first starting Renaissance.

Mary remembers, "We couldn't afford to pay Johnny a salary when we first started the company. When money was so tight, Johnny just lived with us and became part our family. His death was extremely hard for Mike. In part, it was for Johnny and the family that he left behind that Mike carried on and built Renaissance, The Tax People."

It's that kind of personal persistence that is a trademark of Michael Cooper. Mary agrees, "I have never ever, ever known anyone more persistent than Mike. When Mike and I met, I was 18. He was 25. I was a college student. He was widowed with two children.

"Sure, my first reaction was that I liked this guy. I knew he was going places. He called for a date every week for four months and each time I said, 'No.' I know from raising sons of my own how difficult it is for a guy to even ask a girl out the first time. Mike just wouldn't take 'No' for an answer."

During 19 years of marriage and the ups and downs of business, the Coopers have experienced many setbacks, negative experiences and financial struggles as many families do. Mary says with awe, "Mike has never quit. I've said, 'Mike, why don't you just go back to working for someone else?' While I've doubted, he's persisted."

It was in 1984 when Mary and Mike were first introduced to a new way of making money: "We had our first experience with a network marketing company and decided we were going to 'be somebody.' Soon, Mike and I were both presenting on stage in front of crowds. Within months, we were making good money and just knew we were going to be rich! I was so excited to be young and soon-to-be-rich."

A distraught look comes over Mary's face. "It didn't happen. The company suddenly shut its doors and left us out in the cold, like so many other people."

Mary confesses, "I temporarily lost hope in network marketing, but Mike never did. He knew the real power of human potential. His belief in himself and the people who might someday work with him in a solid company kept him going despite my saying, 'Oh honey, do you really think this is what you want to do? Do you really think this will work?'

"One of the reasons this company does work so well is Mike's computer skills. He bought his first computers in the early 1980's before most anyone else did. He was continually upgrading them. Self-taught, he has taken only one computer class in his life. One of the biggest advantages of The Tax People is Mike's ability to develop the software program that runs the entire operation and pays the Independent Marketing

Associates — accurately and on time. I am so proud of him for that."

At a recent Tax People meeting in California, a large audience was in attendance. Mary asked Mike, "What do you think of this crowded room of people? How does it make you feel?"

He looked Mary in the eyes and said, "This is an awesome responsibility."

Mary knows, "Mike is dedicated to all of The Tax People's Independent Marketing Representatives. He is dedicated to the guy working at the bowling alley, the guy running the gas station and the woman who would like to do something different with her life. He knows how you feel because he has been there himself. He will do whatever it takes to make it happen. I am so glad he's my husband and so thankful that he is the president of this company."

During the course of over 200 pages in this book, you've had the opportunity to read the stories of families and individuals whose lives have been changed for the better by The Tax People. Some folks earned more income and others paid fewer taxes, often times both.

Frequently, middle-class families told of permanently finding the answers to their fears of poverty, their lives being brought back from the edges of death. Most believed that no one knew — not their neighbors, not their families, sometimes not even their spouses. They felt all alone with no answers until a message arrived from Michael Cooper.

Here is where this author could play middle-person and recite Michael's message to you. But, I think when building business relationships, it's best to talk one-on-one. I'm sure you'll enjoy the conversation. So here, for the rest of this chapter, is Michael Cooper.

୨ø ༄ႠᏯ ৶৶

Congratulations and thanks for your time. My name is Mike Cooper, President of The Tax People. I wanted to be among the very first to welcome you, maybe even before you have started to use our services.

More than just welcoming you, I wanted to reach out and make sure that I do everything possible to help you reach your goals. One of your goals may be to immediately increase your current take-home pay at your job by $100 each week. You might want to earn $500 or even $5,000 dollars more for your family this month.

If you are experienced in the direct sales industry, this will be your introduction into a radically new concept in marketing. If this is your first exposure to direct sales and networking, then get ready to hang on for the ride of your life. I truly believe that The Tax People could change your life and your financial future for the better.

It's so real that I guarantee in writing that through our Tax Relief System, this company will show you an additional $5,000 in legal deductions or we'll return every penny you paid for our services. That's real. The Tax People is the first and only networking company that absolutely guarantees your success.

My passion is to remove as many stumbling blocks as possible for you, so that the only way you could possibly fail is if YOU choose not to succeed.

At a minimum, you will enjoy several thousand dollars more this year simply by working our business and cutting your taxes. I mean starting this week you can increase your take-home pay. If a few of your friends open their minds, they'll find more money in their pockets as well.

By duplicating our simple story, you can add hundreds, even thousands of additional dollars each week to your family's financial freedom. That can happen fast as well.

But before I go any further, I want to address the ugly of this industry head-on so that you won't think I've had my head buried in the sand. I want you to know that any horror stories you may have heard about this industry are most likely true. I've been with companies that have ripped my heart out. I've been with companies where the owners suddenly became greedy, stupid or both.

I haven't always been proud of our industry. Too many owners and distributors at the top of these companies take the "love'm and leave'm" approach. It disgusts me.

So if you happen to be one of them, do me a favor, and get a refund. I don't want your money. I don't need your money.

The last company I worked with made me president of nothing. They had a dead company. I worked with several other people to re-launch their albatrosses. Soon they were earning over $1 million per month with many people making over $20,000 per month. I was one of them.

Based on this quick success, the owners became instant experts. Their greed and ignorance became known when they changed the proven programs, much to the detriment of people in the field. They were going to pay less, charge more and tell lies to rationalize this to the people that were making them successes, people like you and me and our friends.

Well, just like you, my personal credibility and honor is not for sale. I walked out. In one situation, I was earning over $40,000 per month and resigned as president.

I then founded Renaissance, the parent company of The Tax People. My goal was to create a real corporation with real opportunities, real products and real income for people like us — now and for generations to come.

My goal and mission since day one has been to help more people than any other company in history. You have no idea how it humbles me to see that dream becoming a reality!

Today we have a rock-solid corporation with a board of directors that reads like a Fortune 500 company. We are still in the infancy stage and have more hills to climb, but we will climb them together.

From our little start in 1995, we have built a multi-million dollar company. We identified the single most salable product in America: a system for families to legally, morally and ethically cut their income taxes. Sales have increased 1,200%.

Our business system can show every single person in the country how to cut their taxes and put thousands of dollars back in their pockets. You now have the ability, and I'm going to take it one step further, the responsibility and obligation to show this to every single person you know. You can make them listen to how they can benefit.

For the first time ever, you don't have to worry about being too pushy. In fact, the number one concern should be how pushy can you become. If you had an absolutely safe, proven cure for cancer, and people you loved had it, you'd make them take it even if you had to drag them screaming and kicking. You would not let them die, if you could help.

Right at this moment, there are over 120,000,000 families dying of tax cancer, bill-payment cancer, and no-family-time cancer. You now have the cure. Make them listen.

Millions and millions of Americans are struggling financially. They are in debt up to their elbows and desperately trying to survive their monthly payment cycles. As a result, they are missing out on the most important parts of their families' growth and paying too high a price with in excess of over fifty percent divorce rates from the stress.

Wanting more material things or to give more to your church or help others does not cause the stress. Fighting this battle with no hope of winning causes the strain and frustration.

We all know that money will not buy happiness; but then neither will poverty. In families, lack of money is one of the two most common causes of fights, unhappiness and ultimate divorce. Let's solve the money problem first. You'll at least be able to see the possibilities of a much happier life. We can help you do that.

Instead of being a tax-filing firm that services its clients once a year by collecting money for the IRS, we are helping people day-by-day, week-by-week throughout the year. We position each of our customers with the best possible tax strategy available by law for their individual situations. Our customers pay the minimal taxes allowable by law. There is no gray area. It's legal, black-and-white, found right in the United States tax code and regulations. That's why we also provide tax training for affiliate professionals.

As a nation, America needs a revenue system. If we don't pay enough taxes, the government goes broke. If we overpay our taxes, we go broke. It is a fine balance. The government provides taxpayers with legal tax breaks to help maintain this balance. These tax incentives help direct taxpayers' actions in the best economic interest of the country.

Notice that the government gives substantial tax breaks to people who start businesses. Why is that? Businesses are the backbone of strong economic spending and growth. Our government actually makes money by giving away tax deductions. It may appear that the government is losing money but they are actually gaining it.

Even though it seems our government is taxing income, it is really taxing spending. Your earned income, once spent, becomes someone else's income and spending. At each step, the government collects taxes based on an average tax rate of fifteen percent. That money is taxed each time it flows from your paycheck to the grocer, dry cleaners and auto company.

After seven steps, the government has absorbed almost all of the income through taxes. Each one of us may only pay 10-40% tax on our income, but through this system, 100% of the money eventually goes back into the government system. It then goes back out to the people again in the form of government social programs, highways and schools. Then, they collect tax on it again and again. The cycle continues.

The more money they can entice consumers into spending, the more opportunity the government has to collect taxes. The quicker they can entice people to spend, the quicker the government will increase its income through taxes.

The result is money and it happens when millions of taxpayers initially save billions in taxes. They have more money to spend. They start paying off their credit cards and mortgages. They buy more cars, refrigerators and food. Merchants have more income for the government to tax.

The government wins at every step. Home-based businesses initially create a tax saving which provides people with more money to spend. We've seen why the government likes to create spending.

Then, home business owners can increase their families' incomes. Again, taxes are paid.

The only losers are the people without home-based businesses. They just pay and pay and pay taxes, without ever receiving either the tax benefits or the increased income.

People can change that by starting TTP businesses for as little as $125. We offer a written guarantee that says if we don't find people an additional $5,000 in deductions during their first year in business, we will refund every single penny they paid us.

The Tax People businesses are the only business opportunity that I am aware of which guarantees people will come out ahead. On average, the tax strategies increase people's take-home pay by $300 to $400 a month or more.

It boils down to the question, "What happens if I enroll my mother, my minister and my very best friend as customers of The Tax People? What if they all failed miserably as salespeople and never earned one check from TTP?" The worst case scenario for customers of The Tax People is that they are able to keep on average $5,000 or more in their pockets which they otherwise would have paid in taxes.

People understand and agree. The Tax People customer base is growing at about 23% per month. We've gone from a company that grossed $3,000,000 for the entire year of 1998 to a company grossing over $3,000,000 per month in 1999. That's an annualized income of $36,000,000 over a one-year period of time. By the end of 2000, our annualized revenues are projected to be about $100,000,000.

Project that growth rate out three to five years and we are a billion-dollar company. Even right now, we are the largest and fastest growing non-franchised tax service in America.

During 1998, our gross income projections were surpassed because of the talent, energy and enthusiasm of our Independent Marketing Associates and staff. A couple weeks before Christmas 1998, we hosted a nationwide conference call to announce Christmas bonuses.

These were bonuses sent out to Independent Marketing Associates who had produced certain sales levels. These bonuses were over and above The Tax People's compensation plan. On the conference call I told them, "You don't have to do anything for the money. You've already done it. You helped this company make a profit this year. We're going to give you a bonus."

I promise you that in the history of network marketing, no one knowingly and voluntarily over-pays distributors. It just hasn't happened, until now. The most other companies do is send checks according to their pay plan.

Christmas 1998 found unexpected bonus checks in the hands of 150 Independent Marketing Associates who had enrolled 18 or more new customers for The Tax People's services during the year. Checks for hundreds of dollars started unexpectedly arriving in our Independent Marketing Associates mailboxes. It was my way of saying, "Just go out and have a wonderful Christmas."

My return was ten-fold when the commitment from our Independent Marketing Associates increased annual company revenues from $3 million to $30 million in less than one year.

If people invest in other people properly, the returns will be multi-fold. I invested in furthering the belief of our Independent Marketing Associates that this company is different than any other. We are profitable and here for the long run. I want my Independent Marketing Associates to know in their hearts that they can count on The Tax People being in business ten years from now. I want them to know first-hand that I'm not greedy nor would I ever take advantage of them.

Again during Christmas 1999, we gave over 500 Independent Marketing Associates a total of over $300,000 in holiday bonuses. This included representatives with nine or more sales. Some people had joined in December, sold nine Tax Relief Systems and received a holiday bonus.

Why would I give away $300,000 if I was in this just for myself?

I want 100,000 millionaires with me at the top of this company as The Tax People becomes a multi-billion-dollar corporation.

When I take my last dying breath, I won't be thinking of another million or two that I could have made. I don't want people waiting to throw dirt on my face before the casket is closed. On my last breath, I want to be thinking about all the families who are living financial freedom because of this opportunity.

When I refer to financial independence I don't mean yachts and planes or any of that stuff. I'm talking about having your home, cars and bills paid, not owing a penny to anyone. If you wanted to take off tomorrow to the Bahamas just because you feel like it, you could without worry of how much you'd spend or where the money would come from.

Financial freedom means a debt free lifestyle, lives with enough income to enjoy all of the needs, some of the wants, and some of the charitable aspects of the American Dream with enough money put away that you no longer worry about your future needs. That, my friend, is financial freedom.

It takes income, a lot of income, to reach financial freedom. Let me share with you my philosophy on income. It's centered on the numbers "3" or "4."

For example: Whether you make $30,000 or $40,000 per year, for the average family today, neither income level today will support the American Dream. At $30,000 to $40,000 per year, we would never achieve financial freedom. Of course, any of us could survive on either income level, but we could never enjoy a debt-free life and worry-free retirement.

Although I could be a success as a father, husband and person, earning either number, $30,000 or $40,000 per year means guaranteed failure at achieving the American Dream. So it doesn't matter whether the income is "3" or "4" at this level, because NEITHER level is acceptable for our long-term family desires.

Now let's talk about another "3" or "4." If you could earn $300,000 or $400,000 per year, either income level would support the American Dream. Either would allow a great home, wonderful vacations and the best schools and medical care for your family.

In addition, I think that either number, $300,000 or $400,000 per year is more than enough for your family's desires plus supporting your personal belief system through charitable or humanitarian causes.

I think life would work well at either number, although we would all prefer $400,000 to ONLY $300,000. I think either you or I could live happily with either number, couldn't we?

So once again, it doesn't matter whether the income is "3" or "4" at this level, because EITHER level is acceptable for our long term desires for our families.

Here is a final "3" or "4." If you ever have the opportunity to earn $3,000,000 or $4,000,000 per year, not only have you achieved the American financial Dream, but you have an absolute obligation to share copious amounts of that success with the people and country that made that level of financial success possible for you.

So once again, it doesn't matter whether the income is "3" or "4" at this level, because either of these income levels will generate wealth for your family, your children and your grandchildren for generations to come.

Rich DeVoss, the owner of Amway, created such a legacy. Over the past 40 years, he built a billion-dollar company. He has helped a couple hundred other families earn over a million-dollars as well. His pay plan made him one of the richest men in America, worth $9 or $10 billion at last count. He is rich beyond imagination.

He's getting up in years now. One day he will pass into the hereafter, as we all will. Do you think it is a possibility that his last earthly thought might be, "Gee, I wish I had made just one more billion, that I had made 11 billion instead of 10?"

On our final day, on our final breath, I don't think we will wish for more money. I don't think we will wish we had worked one more day. I do think we will wish that we had spent more time on the important things, our family and friends, thinking of the additional good we could have accomplished for the world.

At the final exit point, what would we do with another billion, even if we had it? Why ever try to accumulate that much wealth in the first place?

If Rich DeVoss had shared over 10% of his company revenues with the people that helped build that company, I'd agree that he might not be worth $9 or $10 billion today — maybe only $300 to $400 million. Only "3" or "4" hundred million. A personal tragedy, huh? However, instead of helping a couple of hundred people become millionaires, he could have created almost 10,000 of them.

Bill Gates is worth about $40 billion. With my philosophy, he might only be worth a billion or two but could have created over 25,000 millionaire families by sharing more of his company with the people that helped build it.

I do think we have a billion dollar company. It is only a matter of time — two years, five years, maybe ten. It depends on how long it takes to reach enough good people like you, people who believe as I do, that "3" or "4" doesn't matter. I don't want your money. I don't need your money. I not only want us to succeed together; I refuse to succeed without you.

Once we succeed together in building this billion dollar company, I may not be one of the wealthiest men in America, but I will surely be one of the richest in all of the important things. On my last breath, I'll be saying, "I'm glad I had a great life, a great time with my family and a great time with my friends."

I won't care at that point, on my last breath, whether I have either a "3" or "4" of any income level. Instead, I will thank the Lord that I was able to help thousands of families enjoy the American Dream.

Conclusion

"It takes as much energy to wish as it does to plan."

— **Eleanor Roosevelt**

Twelve questions to ask yourself:

1) Are you interested in an immediate and on-going increase your net take-home pay averaging $100 or more each week?

2) Would you like to legally lower your income taxes?

3) Would you want your accountant to guarantee you an additional $5,000 in deductions this year?

4) Would you like a protective shield, more powerful than a CPA or accountant, between you and the IRS?

5) Would you like complete audit protection meaning that if the IRS or state tax agency want to audit any tax return, that you will not have to talk to them? Instead, America's most powerful taxpayer advocacy organization comprised of former IRS agents who have turned pro-taxpayer would represent you.

6) If you or anyone you know has IRS collection problems, would you like them favorably resolved?

7) Would you like to earn money working from home on a part-time or full-time basis?

8) Do you want more time to devote to your family?

9) Do you want to be in control of your day-by-day schedule?

10) Did you think that you'd be making more money by this time in your life?

11) Due to retirement, job loss or severe health issue, do you worry how your family would live?

12) Do you want more money to save or invest?

If you answered "yes" to any of the above questions, contact the person whose name appears below or who sent you this book.